Fables, Labels, and Folding Tables

Reflections on the Student Affairs Profession

RANDY L. MITCHELL

Atwood Publishing
Madison, WI

Fables, Labels, and Folding Tables:
Reflections on the Student Affairs Profession
by Randy L. Mitchell
© 1999 by Atwood Publishing
2710 Atwood Ave.
Madison, WI 53704
All rights reserved.

Printed in the United States of America.
02 01 00 99   8 7 6 5 4 3 2 1

Front cover photograph by William Longmoor.

Cover and text design ©1999
by Tamara L. Dever, TLC Graphics.

Library of Congress Cataloging-in-Publication Data
Mitchell, Randy L., 1954 –
        Fables, labels, and folding tables: reflections on the student affairs
        profession/Randy L. Mitchell.
            p.   cm.
        ISBN 1-891859-27-7

        1. Student affairs services—United States. I. Title.

    LB2342.9M58 1999
    378.1'94—dc21   99-21739
                                                             CIP

For the students who instructed me,
the teachers who endured my questions,
the colleagues who crystallized my experiences,
and the mentors who gave me voice.

R.L.M. 1997

Fables can be false or true
or something in between,
but mostly they're another way
to say just what we mean.
Our stories help us understand
but only if they're told,
so here are just a few of mine,
if I might be so bold.

Labels can be right or wrong
or something in between,
and we must read between
*   the lines*
to know what labels mean.
Words are simply metaphors
for feelings, thoughts,
*   and things;*
define the labels in your life
and give your language wings.

Folding tables symbolize
the tools of our trade;
the things we move from
*   place to place,*
the things that give us aid.

And if we use our tools
*   with skill,*
resourcefulness, and pride,
they'll help us reach the
*   ones we teach*
(who teach us on the side).

If you're a chosen member of
a personal profession,
you need to give yourself
*   the gift*
of purposeful reflection.
This book may help you
*   get in touch*
with your own folding tables,
and help you redefine yourself,
your labels and your fables.

Words are simply metaphors
for feelings, thoughts,
*   and things;*
reclaim the wonder in
*   your world*
and give your spirit wings.

Table of Contents

Cloud Watching 101

WHEN I was an undergraduate math major at Florida State University, I took only one psychology course. To this day, I vividly remember a cartoon in my psychology textbook of a small boy helping his father shovel snow after a blizzard. The father is observed saying, "It used to snow lots more when I was a kid." He does not even notice his small, knee-high son struggling to even see over the snowbank behind him.

I remember that cartoon both because I grew up in Florida — I had never seen snow and it fascinated me — and because it illustrated a chapter on "Perception" and helped me learn the various frames, worldviews, and perspectives that different observers bring to the same facts. In my developmental stage at that point, it never occurred to me that people did not see things the way I did.

Why is it that one hall director sees a floor water fight as a battleground and another sees it as a misguided community-building activity? Why is it that someone sees a new job task as an imposition and another sees it as a reward? What is happening when one student sees the red editing marks all over her paper as criticism and the teacher sees it as helpful feedback? Why is it that one mother sees her child misbehaving as a problem and another mother sees it as a teaching opportunity?

The ability to reframe the "obvious" to bring it new meaning is a gift. The ability to see outside the box is vision. The ability to peel away layers of meaning to seek more transcendent truth, or value, or principle, is insight. The ability to understand experience so profoundly to come to new levels of meaning is wisdom.

Randy Mitchell is wise and gifted. His abilities to reframe, to see outside the box, to peel away layers, and to understand his experience is a gift to us all. He can take the most mundane experience and, as a storyteller, use it to see new meaning. I might even find different meaning in his experiences than did he, but that, after all, is perception.

Storytellers are an important part of many cultures. People who can spin tales and draw life lessons from their fables contribute to our learning and our spirit in unfathomable ways. I resonate with writers who can weave metaphors to bring their points to life, who have language to help me see something differently, and who write so engagingly that it makes me want to get a fresh cup of coffee and settle down to read more. Our field has come to value interpretive work and the value of phenomenology. The value of one's lived experience when wise-fully written has transferability to many and lessons for all.

I do not know the process Randy used in writing this book; we have not talked about it. But I do profoundly know that Randy had to allow himself the time to think and reflect. He had to value sitting back and pondering an event, a word, an experience to mine it for the new meanings.

We all need the capacity to write this kind of book. Few of us have the ability currently to do so. As I so often say in speeches, it would benefit all of us to enroll next term in a course called "Cloud Watching 101." All you have to do if you want to pass the course is literally or figuratively lay on the grass and stare at the clouds for a half-hour, three times a week.

Could you pass this course? Many of you could and know you need that kind of reflective time to center yourself, to regain your energy, and to get perspective. Others of us cannot even imagine that kind of alone time. We'd worry that we'd have nothing to say to ourselves and that we'd have a thousand things we could do with that precious time.

But the ability to calmly reflect may be one of the most underdeveloped of professional skills. Reflection helps us work smarter; reflection helps bring our values into our actions; reflection brings our private self into our professional self; reflection helps us gain perspective on our priorities.

Even if you find reflection hard, you will learn to do it a bit better by reading one of the essays in this book with your morning coffee. Or read an essay in bed at night. Or turn to an essay that relates to a similar experience you're having, so that you might see it differently.

With this book and in his life, Randy has not only passed "Cloud Watching 101" — he gets an A+.

– Susan R. Komives

Susan R. Komives is an Associate Professor of Counseling and Personnel Services, teaching in the College Student Personnel Administration program at the University of Maryland, College Park. A former President of the American College Personnel Association and former Vice President of both Stephens College and the University of Tampa, she is co-author of *Exploring Leadership: For College Students Who Want to Make a Difference* and co-editor of *Student Services*.

Acknowledgments

I've long believed that one of humanity's greatest gifts is inspiration. Not only can we build tools, make language, and use our thumbs — we can also inspire one another to think, act, dream, create, and believe. The "fables," "labels," and "folding tables" in this book might be mine, but the work and words of some incredible people influenced many of these ideas.

It's impossible to think about student transition without paying homage to John Gardner (University of South Carolina). His written works and personal presentations — and those of his staff — offer a strong foundation for thinking about the freshman year. John's seminars and presentations have become nothing short of legendary in the world of student success, academic advising, and enrollment management.

Rick Miller (Designs for Development) has been providing interesting metaphors for leadership for more than ten years, first from a higher education base and now in consulting. His "elixir" on leadership transformed into one of my "leadership recipes" (he doesn't mind that I borrowed some of his ingredients to prepare my entrée ...).

My erstwhile employee, current colleague, faithful friend, and presentation partner, Lee Ward (James Madison University), continues to instruct me in the finer points of student learning and role ambiguity. Through him I've been exposed to the leadership taxonomies of George Kuh (Indiana University) and the planned change models of Don Creamer (Virginia Tech).

I've learned through personal experience that none of them will ever amount to much in the game of horseshoes.

An American Imperative: Higher Expectations for Higher Education inspired the "Student Learning Imperative" of the American College Personnel Association, which inspired the student success program at James Madison University, which inspired my involvement in many of the activities chronicled in this book. Though I'm not acquainted with the authors of *An American Imperative*, I'd like to acknowledge their role in creating a new, collaborative vision for learning and higher education.

You can't be married to someone for over twenty years without her (or his) professional interests harmonizing with your own. Deb Mitchell, my wife, constant companion, and favorite interior decorator influences my thinking about physical environments. Without her, I couldn't tell a "double rub" from a "lambrekin" (literally and figuratively)!

Thoughts, ideas, and quotes from authors, poets, songwriters, and other thinking people appear throughout the book. Though they may never get all the credit they're due, I've tried to the best of my ability to credit them when and where appropriate.

My everlasting thanks and appreciation are extended to the friends and colleagues who reviewed early drafts of this book. The invaluable insights and constructive criticism of Ruth Bradford Burnham (Bucknell University), Linda Moore (University of North Carolina at Wilmington), Mark Warner (James Madison University), and Suzanne Straub (James Madison University) helped me recount the fables, reveal the labels, and unfold the tables. And my most grand "thank you" is reserved for the best assistant in the whole wide world, Judy Marshall.

R . L . M .

About This Book

Who Should Read This Book?

- New professionals encountering some of the challenges inherent in the student affairs profession (*they didn't tell me this in grad school!*);

- Seasoned student affairs professionals engaged in generative activity, looking for some new angles on old issues (*let me explain it another way...*);

- Graduate students or prospective graduate students pursuing a career in student affairs (*you mean people get paid to do this?*).

Why Should You Read This Book?

The student affairs profession is complex and dynamic, as old as higher education and as new as today's headlines. Sometimes, the profession's complexity and dynamism obstruct our ability as professionals to see clearly, speak clearly, and make sense out of our daily trials, tribulations, and triumphs. We have access to a great deal of literature on *how* to do what we do, but we rarely talk about *why* we do what we do. Though our profession has rich theoretical underpinnings, we seem less sure of our philosophical foundations. We spend significant amounts of time, money, and energy in developing the technology related to our profession; how much do we spend on developing the *humanity* of our profession?

If we don't purposefully share our stories, reclaim our language, and develop our capacity to use our tools, our profession is in jeopardy of losing its relevance in the changing world of higher education.

The essays in this book are my way of examining and transforming the humanity of the student affairs profession. Each essay falls (loosely) under one or more of the themes in the book's title: *fables*, *labels*, and *folding tables*. *Fables* are simply stories and experiences that provide potential direction for the profession. *Labels* capture the names and ways used to describe people, movements, causes, and paradigms; labels can help or hinder our communication. *Folding tables* is a theme used to illustrate our need for tools, symbols, and physical surroundings — the tricks and tools of our trade.

By reading this book and employing the questions posed in each essay for personal reflection and group discussion, you will have the opportunity to:

- Discover your own *fables* so that your work will have greater value and deeper meaning for you and those with whom you work.

- Discover — and possibly reframe — the *labels* used to describe you, the labels you use to describe others, and the language we use with varying degrees of effectiveness in our profession.

- Discover your own *folding tables*, so that you can become more resourceful and more skilled about the needs and expectations of our profession.

How to Read This Book

Although we've been taught from an early age to read a book from start to finish, the essays in this book are intended to be enjoyed and considered individually, and not necessarily in the order in which they appear. As you would with a cookbook, find a recipe you like and use it more than once. Experiment with different recipes. Mix and match — an appetizer here, a main course there, a light dessert for later. You know best how much you can digest in one sitting.

Music is an art in which fables, labels, and folding tables come together. Songs are fables in lyrical form, laden with labels and meaning, more portable than the best folding table. That's why each essay in this book begins with a song quote. My thanks to the many writers and musicians who provide the "soundtracks to our lives" (a line from songwriter Mac McAnally). A frustrated, unpublished songwriter, I've included a few lyrics of my own. Your responsibility as a reader is to think of additional songs, books, films, or paintings that might help to illustrate your own fables, labels, and folding tables.

This book is not a handbook for the profession, a checklist of essential habits or skills, or a thesis based on statistical research. It is primarily a reflection on personal experience, intended to help you reflect on your own personal experience. Each essay concludes with three questions for discussion or personal reflection. If other questions arise as you read or discuss, even better.

There's more to each essay than is revealed in its title; I've stubbornly refused to force the essays exclusively into any of the three themes. In the appendix of the book, however — the "Table of Context" — I've listed categories of reflection questions, along with the essays in which the questions appear. If you prefer, start with the reflection questions in mind, then select the essays that set up the questions.

If, however, you insist on reading the book from start to finish, I'll try to understand!

What You Will Discover in This Book

- Where to find treasures in the student affairs profession.
- What geese can teach us about leadership.
- How driving, auto maintenance, and road conditions are related to organizational direction.
- Whether you should wear the Cape of Good Hope or Cape Fear.
- How imagination transforms our work.
- Why everyone holds an "acting" position.
- How roles differ from responsibilities.
- What it means to be a director or a leader.
- How to work without a net.
- What collaboration really means.
- How air conditioning applies to people conditioning.
- What your double-rub potential is.
- How to pass metaphorical stones.
- What kind of floor you are.
- How painting a room can provide personal balance.
- How to see through your windows.
- Why you should build sandcastles.

I truly hope that *Fables, Labels, and Folding Tables* makes you think, inspires you to reflect, and reminds you why you do the things you do. I also hope it helps you in your work with students and in the other areas of your life. I invite and encourage you to contact me and share your feedback; I'd love to hear about your fables, labels, and folding tables. My e-mail address is: mitcherl@jmu.edu

Enjoy!
R.L.M.

Sandcastles

"And so castles made of sand

Slip into the sea

Eventually."

JIMI HENDRIX

IMAGINE a 43-year-old man, overweight and sporting three days' growth on a full beard, wearing baggy swim trunks, his pale skin shining like a beacon much whiter than the sand surrounding him. Wallowing in moist sand, he meticulously sculpts an intricate, multi-layered sandcastle on a southern North Carolina beach.

A near euphoric expression covers his face as each level takes shape. He drills windows into the sand escarpments with a dried stalk of sea oat. He uses his children's sandcastle forms to build towers and to enhance the battlements. Oblivious to the late-afternoon sun and the impending tide, he builds his castle, a temporary and regal monument. Thoughts of work, debts, and the latest Washington, D.C., scandal couldn't be farther from his consciousness. He completes his castle moments before the tide fills his man-made moat. Within the next ten minutes, his work will be washed away.

I repeat this ritual each August.

Sometimes, my daughters assist with the construction if they're not engaged in creating their own short-lived shrines. More often, I'm an independent contractor. I'm a freestyle sand architect: no blueprints or plans exist on paper or in my mind. I start to dig the moat, piling the sand in the middle until it forms an adequate mound. Then, I begin to carve. There is no symmetry to my work, and right angles are rarely employed. I work with the mass I've created, follow my instincts, and come up with some — perhaps interesting is the best word — conceptions.

Sometimes I write this way as well. I'm doing so now.

Anyway, I don't regret the loss of the castles when they're swept away by the changing tides. If anything, I've come to appreciate and enjoy this temporary chef d'oeuvre. It costs so little if I'm already at the beach. It brings me joy for a little while, but joy's like that. It reminds me that, in a way, everything I do is like building sandcastles.

I understand that Buddhists and certain southwestern Native American tribes specialize in sand painting. They create magnificent, resplendent, intricate works of art. These masterpieces aren't conceived to last forever. They become gifts to the winds.

Sandcastles are my gifts to the sea.

———

Sad? Yes and no.

We make impressions — some longer-lasting than others. We leave footprints, for awhile. Time, the wind, and those who follow often erase our impressions and muddle our footprints.

It's OK. Really. That's the way it works.

This summer, I sat in my beach chair at the water's edge in a late-afternoon haze, my feet digging a lagoon in the sand. I focused on the sounds of the surf, silently watching my daughters as they built their own sandcastles to my right and left. My oldest daughter, recently graduated from high school and college-bound, her face obscured by dangling, wind-blown hair, played in the sand as she'd done for the last eighteen years. Her youngest sister excavated her own sand quarry nearby.

In a magical moment, cast forever in time and in my soul, I realized that they too were sandcastles — wonderful, beautiful, intelligent, incredible, living sandcastles.

In that moment, I appreciated the short, sweet wonder of knowing that they too would shine in the sun for a fleeting instant, then be swept away by the tide of time. My role in their development was almost over; they would take their own shape in other places, at other times, creating their own moments and monuments in the sun.

Sad? Yes and no.

Someone once said that our children are only on loan to us. Kahlil Gibran, in *The Prophet*, suggested that our children are living arrows and that we are the bows. The things we love are not ours to keep.

It's OK. Really. That's the way it works.

The campus construction projects I've been involved in over the past twenty years are sandcastles — expensive and lasting a little longer than those on the beach, but sandcastles nonetheless.

Time, the wind, and those who follow often erase our impressions.

The programs and services I've helped develop are sandcastles. Some have already gone to sea: others have a strong foothold on the beachhead.

We leave footprints, for awhile. These too shall pass.

The students and staff members I've worked with are sandcastles. They too take their own shape in other places, at other times.

They become our gifts to the world.

We can mourn the passage of our sandcastles: it's an essential stage in the process of living and learning. We can try to protect the castles, building walls and levees around them. But somehow, the tide always finds its way through our barriers. We can shout that it's not fair, that the things we build and the things we love ought to last forever.

Or, we can learn to appreciate and enjoy our temporary masterpieces. We can build our buildings, create our programs, and contribute to the development of our students and staffs — for now.

We can understand that it's OK. Really. That's the way it works.

I'll miss my daughter when she goes away to college. I've already begun the mourning, but I'm beginning to celebrate her adulthood as well. These two emotions are compatible. No wall or levee is going to stop her from becoming the wonderful woman that she's been becoming for the past eighteen years. She's one of my gifts to the world.

I only hope that she'll continue to build sandcastles, literally and figuratively.

I mourn when staff members go on to sometimes bigger and sometimes better opportunities, but I celebrate their choices as well. These two emotions are compatible.

I celebrate the success and graduation of students — who are the very reason why I'm in this profession — even as I hate to see them leave (well, most of them anyway).

After giving birth to a new facility or program, I have the postpartum blues. It's a natural reaction. But before long, a new facility or program takes its place.

Every day, we build sandcastles. Every day, some of them are washed away. It's OK. Really. That's the way it works.

REFLECTION

1) What are some examples of sandcastles you've built, and what brought them down?

2) When should sandcastles be protected from the tides? Why?

3) How could you use the sandcastle metaphor as a training tool for students or staff?

Folding Tables

"In a world filled with people,

Only some want to fly;

Isn't that crazy?"

SEAL

THE human race. An evolutionary enigma. Capable of so much good. Capable of so much evil. Highly developed in the manipulation of its environment. Able to build and utilize tools. Able to think, create, destroy, and create again. Inventive.

We think, therefore we invent.

What comes to mind when you think of the great inventions of the human race? The wheel? The printing press? Penicillin? Electricity? The internal combustion engine? The telephone? The radio? Nuclear fission? Microchips? Lasers?

Too easy.

Sure, all of these developments were important. Life as we know it was and continues to be shaped by inventions like these.

But think smaller for a moment. Think of inventions that are so much a part of your life that you take them totally for granted. Now, think what your life would be like without them.

Paper clips. Not very significant, right? How about fingernail clippers? Scissors? Swiss Army knives? Pencil sharpeners? Velcro? Forks? Combs? Keys?

If we didn't have them, we'd have to invent them.

Folding tables. Not very important — unless you have to feed five hundred people in a hurry in a room where you also need to sell books, hold career fairs, sponsor dances, and show movies.

Believe it or not, there can be wonder in the mundane, magic in the ordinary, and wisdom in the commonplace.

Who are the inventors of these simple solutions? We generally don't know. The first person to take a wire and bend it into a paper clip probably didn't get rich. There is no nail clipper king to my knowledge. Henrico Scissors is not commemorated on a stamp. Yet these are examples of human ingenuity.

Much of the human experience related to discovery goes unrecognized. In a world filled with things, we take things for granted. In a world filled with ideas, we take ideas for granted. In a world filled with people, we take people for granted.

Like folding tables, we put them away when we're finished with them.

———◦◦———

In higher education, we have a unique opportunity to *not* take things, ideas, and people for granted. We have the opportunity to examine more closely, to listen to more loudly, and to sense more fully the world we inhabit and the worlds we create. If we don't — and if we don't teach our students to experience their lives more completely — then we've wasted the precious gifts of time, money, and human energy allocated to us.

On a campus filled with students, only some want to learn; isn't that crazy? How can we help our students experience their lives more completely? We can help them learn to reflect on their experiences. We can help them identify and learn to use the tools they will need to be successful in all aspects of their lives. We can help them nurture their own creativity and innovation rather than stifling these qualities through policies, procedures, and rules. We can help them discover their own human ingenuity, with hopes that they will be the inventors of the 21st century. We can help them learn to make connections between study, work, and play. We can teach them to examine more closely, listen more loudly, and sense more fully the world they inhabit — through our programs, services, mentoring relationships, and other interactions.

———◦◦———

A custodian taught me several years ago that much less pressure would be placed on my hands if I carried a folding table by its folded legs rather than by the metal edge of the tabletop. A simple lesson perhaps, but one that saved me a substantial degree of discomfort. He was just one of the many teachers I had in college; he knew how to use his tools and how to teach others to use them.

I recently bought an eight-foot, commercial-quality folding table for use at home. To date, we've used the table for a garage sale, for a neighborhood picnic, as a temporary desk, as a fabric-cutting surface for our daughter's Evil Stepmother costume, and as a place to stack books while painting a room. It's made me wonder how we possibly managed a household without a folding table.

Folding tables may just be *things* — instrumental and practical. But with a little creativity and ingenuity, they take on more magical, spiritual qualities. Thomas Moore, in his bestselling book, *Care of the Soul*, suggests that things have soul; that the value of things is based on our attachment to them and the meanings and memories those things have in our lives. Moore concludes by speculating on whether things can suffer, not unlike people, when they have no value or meaning beyond their function.

How often do the things, ideas, and people that cross our paths in student affairs suffer because we see them only as instrumental, practical, and functional?

This essay began with the words from a Seal song, "Crazy." *"In a world filled with people, only some want to fly; isn't that crazy?"* I think it's crazy to not find wonder in the mundane, magic in the ordinary, and wisdom in the commonplace.

In a world filled with things, let's not take things for granted. In a world filled with ideas, let's not take ideas for granted. In a world filled with people, let's not take people for granted. Let's encourage them to fly.

REFLECTION

1) What are some of the ways in which you help your students experience their lives more fully?

2) What are some of the folding tables/inventions/resources that are critical to your personal and professional success in student affairs? Why?

3) How might we more effectively value things, ideas, and people beyond their function?

Professional Acting

"No man's a jester playing Shakespeare
Round your throne room floor
While the juggler's act is danced upon
The crown that you once wore."

ELTON JOHN AND BERNIE TAUPIN

I'VE held an acting position for the past several months — "Acting Associate Vice President of Student Affairs for Enrollment Services," to be exact. Someone once said that if it takes more than three words to identify your position, you're probably not necessary. Maybe that person was right. Getting all of those words onto a calling card or a letterhead — not to mention trying to answer the telephone — is a challenge. By the time readers or callers are finished with your title, they've forgotten why they wanted to talk to you in the first place.

Actually, the most important word in my title, as it turns out, is "acting."

Acting ...

"I'm not a real associate vice president of student affairs for enrollment services, but I play one on TV."

———

Try explaining to your kids that you have an acting position:

"What's your job again, Dad?"

"Well, I'm the acting associate vice president of student affairs for enrollment services."

"Gee, Dad, does that mean you can get us free theater tickets?"

"Well, no, I'm not actually working with the theater department."

"But you *said* you were the *acting* associate whatever..."

"That's not what it means. The acting part means I'm *doing* the job but I don't actually *have* the job."

"You're doing a job you don't have to do?"

"No, no. I have to do the job, but I'm not officially *in* the job."

"Either you have a job or you don't. What are you saying, Dad? Does this mean I won't be able to go to college? *Mom*!"

———•◦•———

Try explaining to other relatives that you have an acting position:

"How's work?"

"Great. I was recently appointed as the acting associate vice president of student affairs for enrollment services."

"Sounds impressive. Does that mean you got a promotion?"

"Well, yes and no. I have more responsibility and a much longer title, but it's only temporary."

"For how long?"

"I don't really know for sure."

"Are you being phased out?"

"No, this is actually an opportunity."

"Let me get this straight. You've got more responsibility but no security?"

"Actually, I think it means they like me. They know I can handle it."

"If they know you can handle it, why don't they just give you the job?"

"It's not that easy. There has to be a search, and the position has to be advertised, and if I was interested I'd have to apply."

"You'd have to apply for the job you're already doing?"

"That's right."

"And what part of that makes you think they like you?"

———•◦•———

Try explaining to your former co-workers that you're now their supervisor in an acting capacity:

"Well, it looks like I'll be working with you even more closely now. *(I sure hope they accept me in this new capacity.)*"

"Great. *(Why did he get the nod? I've been here just as long.)*"

"I obviously don't know as much about your area as you do, so I'll have to learn from you. *(I'm a little scared here, but I can't show it.)*"

"No problem. You'll be up to speed on all of this in no time. *(Great. Now I've got to do my job and his!)*"

"I have no idea how long this assignment will be in effect, but my relationship with you is important. Nothing's going to change. *(Of course everything will change. Like it or not, this is a power relationship, and I'm feeling like I have all of the responsibility here to make it work.)*"

"You can count on me. *(What do you mean, nothing's going to change? You're the person now who has impact on my salary, even on my advancement.)*"

"I'm not going to get in your way. You're the director. I want you to feel that you have the freedom to get the job done. *(In other words, your success or failure has an impact on my success or failure now.)*"

"I'm going to enjoy working with you in this new arrangement. *(I'll make the best of it, but my guard is up. Your success or failure has an impact on my success or failure now.)*"

Fact: *everyone* is in an acting position.

Everyone.

With the possible exception of the Pope, the Supreme Court justices, and certain conservative senators in the Deep South.

Permanence is relative. Reorganization can turn a permanent position on its head. Changing conditions in higher education dictate that permanence is an illusion. Tenure, the standard of permanence in higher education, is under attack. Colleges and universities may not be able to sustain the departmentalized, compartmentalized, specialized approach to education that has defined the last century. Faculty who focus on specialized courses that don't attract sufficient enrollment now find themselves being asked to pick up general education coursework and cross-disciplinary study. They don't like it, but we can't always ignore what we don't like.

Permanence in student affairs is an illusion as well. All of the departments we've created — including the divisions of student affairs, academic affairs, etc. — are constructs. Someone made them up. You won't find them in the Constitution or in any major religious teachings. They were created to meet needs. Needs change, and so must our creations.

We educate our student affairs graduate students to believe that there will always be housing offices, student activities, counseling centers, financial aid offices, and admissions offices, as we know these services today. We tell them to make a choice and to specialize. In effect, though, we may be preparing them for a career that no longer exists.

Instead, we should prepare graduate students to be acting professionals in the field of student affairs. Learn the methods, we should tell them. Learn the role. Learn the script. Understand your character, your fellow actors, your setting, your stage, and your audience. Become the character you've been assigned. Learn the moves. Use the props you've been given. Perform. Don't try to steal the show; you're part of an ensemble. Learn from your mistakes. Then move on to the next role. Try not to be typecast.

In other words, don't limit yourself to being seen only as a programmer or as an operations person; develop skills in both areas. Don't identify exclusively with one department or function; demonstrate competency beyond your assignment. Don't just fill the role you've been assigned; expand it with collaboration, professional development, and innovation.

We all know that there are numerous possibilities for the future. Prediction is an imperfect art, but I can't help speculating. In the very near future, flexibility will be more important than specialty. Breadth will be at least as important as depth. Cross-functional teams will conceivably replace standard departments as the means for achieving outcomes. Organizational charts will be less important than flowcharts. Many of the functions currently conducted by the college or university will be conducted by external organizations. New functions will develop on campus to meet unaddressed needs. In this potential scenario, specialists will be in trouble — just like the faculty members who hang on to the *teaching* of favorite courses at the expense of the *learning* needed by students and by the communities that sent them to college.

We talk of the whole student, but we approach the students as if they're nothing more than sides of beef, divided into quarters and sections with labels like *student affairs*, *academic affairs*, *business affairs*, etc. stenciled on their flanks. The word *division* says it all. We divide education. Shouldn't we instead integrate it? A common mission, common goals, shared resources, and collaborative efforts should be the hallmarks of a quality institution. Student affairs professionals should be held accountable for their cooperative endeavors with professionals from the rest of the academy. And that means going beyond the functional job description.

Although I have struggled with the ambiguity involved, I've learned that acting positions give you the opportunity to strip away *the job* and instead concentrate on *the work*.

What if we all had acting positions? Would we be more likely to focus on learning the necessary skills, making the necessary alliances, and sharing the necessary resources? Is it possible that *what we're called* would be less important than *what we do*? Would we be forced to understand our colleagues' needs? Would we spend more time trying to achieve success and less time trying to explain what got in the way of our success?

Probably not.

People yearn too strongly for permanence, security, and status. Change threatens permanence, security, and status. Nature and universities abhor vacuums, or so I've been told, and sooner or later a new structure would replace the old one. Similar to the logic of Orwell's *Animal Farm*, all people would have acting positions, but some would be more acting than others.

Maybe we can create a hybrid of sorts. Maybe we can take the best qualities of permanence and the best qualities of acting, combining them into a new paradigm of professional behavior. Maybe we could *hold* permanent positions but *act* as if we were in acting positions.

The former president of my university frequently said that he *acted* as if every day was his first day on the campus. He was the president for over 27 years. He was also incredibly innovative and visionary. Not everyone liked or supported all of his actions, but it was difficult to argue with his accomplishments. Perhaps he'd been an *acting* president for 27 years.

The root of *acting* is *act*. Act is a verb; so is work. Jobs are nouns. Did you go to *work* last week or did you go to your *job*? If you're *acting*, you're *doing* something. Forget the theatrical context of acting as pretending: the question should become *to do or not to do* rather than *to be or not to be*.

Maybe it's time each of us *acted* more like the professional we always wanted to be.

REFLECTION

1) How would you distinguish between your work (verb) and your job (noun)? Are you motivated by your work (what you do) or by your job (office, title, compensation, etc.)?

2) If you could create an acting position for yourself, what types of things would you be doing (as opposed to what your title would be, where you would park, what your office would look like, etc.)? How would you act?

3) What can you do to give your current position some of the characteristics described above?

Hope and Fear

"Now we can live in fear
Or act out of hope ..."

JOHN HIATT

WHICH do you wear — the "Cape of Good Hope" or "Cape Fear"?

Are you motivated by hope or by fear? Do you motivate others by hope or by fear? It's a question I've asked others and myself on numerous occasions. The answer to either question — it's generally the same answer for both questions — is perhaps one of the most important things you can know about yourself and others.

There are religions based on hope and religions based on fear — inspiration or condemnation. I grew up in a religion of fear. I migrated to a religion of hope. The minister recently told me, "If my family's in the basement, I can shut off the lights, slam the door, and scare them upstairs. Or I can say to them, 'Come up and see the wonderful banquet that's been laid out for you.'" His ministry appeals to me.

There are relationships based on hope and relationships based on fear — trust or suspicion. I grew up in a family of fear. I've built my own family of hope. I've been a trustworthy father, my wife has been a trustworthy mother, and our children have flourished in the belief that their parents believe in them. We hope that our trust is so strong that it will overcome the missteps, mistakes, and misunderstandings that come with life.

There are organizations based on hope and organizations based on fear — persuasion or control. I started my professional life in a student affairs organization that operated exclusively by threat, intimidation, secrecy, and power. I'm helping to create a student affairs organization that operates through inspiration, collaboration, openness, and influence. There are still missteps, mistakes, and misunderstandings, but a bad day in this environment beats the best of days in the former environment.

Fear may be effective in the short term. You can scare people into doing just about anything — for awhile. But resistance eventually begins to grow: passive, aggressive, or passive-aggressive. Sooner or later, people find the bully's weaknesses. Perhaps a bigger bully comes along. Short-term gains turn into long-term barriers. Motivation by fear breeds contempt.

Hope is more effective in the long term. Inspired people are capable of doing just about anything — and for a long while. The positive energy eventually begins to grow: self-actualizing and self-sufficient. Sooner or later, people find their hopes being realized. Perhaps bigger hopes come along. Long-term gains turn into long-term possibilities. Motivation by hope breeds opportunity.

Hope. Such a hopeful word. Some call it faith or belief; others call it optimism or desire. "Hope springs eternal," Alexander Pope surmised several hundred years ago. Hope is not an empty emotion or an effortless wish; hope requires commitment, purpose, and action. Hope gives you something constructive to do with your energy. Hope gives you strength; fear takes it away.

Student affairs should be a hoping profession. We should provide opportunities for our students and staffs to turn their hopes and dreams into plans and actions. We should instill in our students and staffs a desire to build communities of hope, both on the campus and in the greater community. We should practice hope every day, even in the face of fear. We should read and write more letters, articles, and books that inspire us through their hopeful visions. We should talk with our colleagues and students about hopes and fears; naming fears helps to take away some of their power, and articulating hopes helps to make them real. Hope should be a central theme in our student development, staff development, and student learning efforts.

Are you motivated by hope or by fear? What makes you choose or continue on the path you've chosen? What does your religion offer in the way of inspiration or condemnation? What do your relationships offer in the way of trust or suspicion? What does your organization offer in the way of persuasion or control?

What do you offer in the way of hope or fear?

REFLECTION

1) What are your hopes and fears? With whom do you share them?

2) How do hope and fear affect your interactions with those you supervise? Those who supervise you? Your colleagues?

3) What steps can you and others take to maximize hope and minimize fear in your organization?

Collaboration

"It helps me not to be afraid,
Knowing we're so much the same.
The road we take leads to the stars;
We're just driving different cars."

CAROL JOHNSON

THERE are no enemies in the higher education enterprise: just friends and allies with whom we have yet to collaborate.

In my formative years, I was exposed to numerous movies and television shows about World War II. The Korean "conflict" was never really resolved, and the Vietnam "quagmire" was deepening. I guess we only wanted to celebrate a war that had actually come to a definitive conclusion — a war that we had "won."

The bad guys wore meticulous, gray uniforms, spoke in English with bad German accents (before the dawn of subtitles), were generally cruel, and were somehow less bright than their Allied adversaries. It's hard to imagine villains more evil than Hitler and his minions, although some characters were presented as sympathetic, albeit stupid. Sergeant Schultz and Colonel Klink come to mind.

Worse than the "enemy," by far, were the scoundrels who collaborated with them. These guys — male or female — were the lowest of the low, the vilest of the vile, pond scum on a bad day. You could eventually forgive your foes; no atrocity they visited on you or your friends compared with the evil done by their collaborators. At least that's the way it was on film.

Until much later, I never heard the word collaboration used in anything other than a negative context. The word *collaborating* was always followed by the words *with the enemy.*

Somehow, that notion still lives.

Collaboration in and of itself is anything but negative. Collaboration, according to my tattered 1973 version of *The American Heritage Dictionary of the English Language,* is "1. To work together, especially in joint intellectual effort." But the next reference is "2. To cooperate treasonably."

Although we in higher education periodically give lip service to collaboration as an essential ingredient in planning, goal setting, and the use of resources, our actions suggest that we perceive collaboration through the second definition, cooperative treason. If we go over to the "other side" to attempt cross-divisional, seamless connections, we're guilty of collaborating. If we stretch beyond our own boundaries, learn how the other half lives, and begin to incorporate some of "their" perspective into our own words and actions, we're guilty of collaborating. If we side with one of "them" in a conflict with one of "ours," we're guilty of collaborating.

I know what it's like. I'm one of those people guilty of collaborating. In my case, it's with faculty members.

No, they don't wear meticulous, gray uniforms. If anything, their dress is about as non-uniform as it can be, from flood victim couture to Cosmopolitan chic. No, they don't speak in English with bad German accents — though many of them have authentic accents from various regions and countries. None of them, to my knowledge, is very cruel — except perhaps at midterm. Most of them are as bright as my other colleagues, and a few of them have a bit of an edge on critical thinking skills. I have yet to meet a Sergeant Schultz or a Colonel Klink on our faculty, though they may exist there as well as in other parts of the academy. I've found our faculty to be primarily made up of people who love teaching, learning, and their disciplines.

There are no enemies in the higher education enterprise: just friends and allies with whom we have yet to collaborate.

This perspective frequently gets me in trouble with a few of my non-faculty colleagues. They think that collaborating with people outside the department or division is a sign of weakness. Take care of your own. Cover your organizational ass. Do it for the team. Play your cards close to the vest. Never let 'em see you sweat. To err is human: to forgive is for wimps.

There's an alternative to this perspective — and you can find it by following that first definition of collaboration. I believe we're engaged in joint intellectual effort, and that working together is the surest method for success. I believe departmentalism and divisionalism prevent us from effectively meeting our goals. I believe our students suffer because we don't collaborate as effectively as we could. Through collaboration, the institution has the opportunity to maximize the utilization of resources, eliminate duplication and non-productive competition, and more effectively address the total needs of the student in a comprehensive manner. Through collaboration, the whole is greater than the sum of the parts.

That same old dictionary of mine, incidentally, has an interesting entry for the term *college*: "4. A body of persons having a common purpose or common duties." What a novel concept!

There are no enemies in the higher education enterprise: just friends and allies with whom we have yet to collaborate.

Through a series of retreat discussions and activities, the people I work with recently came up with a definition of what collaboration can and should be:

Collaboration is creating partnerships, across and within departments, based on trust, respect, and commitment for the purpose of achieving organizational and educational goals.

There are three components in this definition: a) creating partnerships across and within departments, b) based on trust, respect, and commitment, and c) for the purpose of achieving organizational and educational goals. If you go deeper into these components, you can begin to define specific, measurable, realistic, and timely actions that result in collaboration. You can begin to remove obstacles and create conditions for collaboration. You can begin to employ collaboration, formally and informally, in your planning process.

The following questions, developed through our team process, may lead to ideas for your organization:

Creating partnerships across and within departments ... . What specific actions must people take to develop partnerships? Is it a joint activity, or must it be individual responsibility, one person at a time, one step at a time? How willing are individuals to take risks, to come together on common issues? How do we recognize and celebrate partnerships when they do take place?

What specific actions must we take to help colleagues get "out of the box?" What tools do people need to get out? How do we help them distinguish between having a full plate (i.e., "My plate is too full") and having a balanced meal (i.e., "I have the right things on my plate")? How do we illustrate our mutual dependence while taking care of security needs and permitting mistakes? When do we take the time to teach others what we do, to learn what they do, and to figure out how we might help one another in the process? Would it help to engage in more out-of-position-description opportunities? How can we best provide and encourage personal and professional growth?

... based on trust, respect, and commitment ... . What specific commitments can we make to communicate more effectively with one another? When do we make time to engage in discussions with others, one on one, out of our "camp"? What is our commitment to follow-up or to go to the source when we hear news, gossip, or innuendo? How do we acknowledge and collectively overcome barriers to collaboration?

What specific actions can we take to reduce the fears of risk taking that accompany collaboration? How do we increase and communicate the real value of collaboration? How do we model collaboration? What interpersonal and community relations must we develop? How do we learn that it's healthy to trust? How do we demonstrate our trustworthiness? What specific commitments can we make to minimize competition among staff, departments, and divisions?

... for the purpose of achieving organizational and educational goals. What specific actions can we take to recognize and reward collaborative efforts? What formal and informal means can we employ? Should collaboration be a key behavioral factor in performance planning and appraisal?

What specific roles should collaboration play in the planning process before goals, objectives, and budgets are developed? How can we "collaborate to plan" and "plan to collaborate"? How can we best look at interdisciplinary opportunities and "the big picture"? How can collaboration provide better information for planning, implementation, and evaluation of goals and outcomes?

Danish poet and artist Piet Hein wrote: "The noble art of losing face may someday save the human race." How many conflicts — global, national, regional, departmental, or personal — are the result of "face saving" being more highly valued than cooperation, collaboration, and mutual benefit?

There are no enemies in the higher education enterprise: just friends and allies with whom we have yet to collaborate.

"To work together, especially in joint intellectual effort." These words should appear in all of our mission statements. If you have an adversarial relationship with someone in your department, division, or institution, try a little collaboration. Lose a little face every now and then.

Face it: what have you got to lose?

REFLECTION

1) How could you best address the questions posed in this essay with a group of students, staff, or peers?

2) Have you ever lost face and saved something more valuable?

3) Who are your potential "friends and allies," and how might you collaborate with them?

So Close

"We never started the world on fire
But we came so close ..."

R.L.M.

"MR. B." He was probably the only teacher I ever really hated. I'm not talking about resentment or fear; I'm talking pure, unadulterated, All-American hate. It was an irrational hatred, to say the least, but it was nonetheless pure. His most frequently abused maxim was, "Close only counts in horseshoes, hand grenades, and herpes." I learned to despise him for those words.

My problem was twofold: I took his geometry course the same year I went out for baseball. It was my tenth-grade year, and I decided to please my father by going out for sports. "Mr. B." was the coach.

As long as I ran my wind sprints, worked hard during practice, and was a team player, my geometry scores were excellent. I appeared to have talent in both arenas, so to speak. For an all-too-short period that spring, the sun was shining on and off the diamond.

Then I dropped out of baseball.

The reason was lost on him. Needing money to help out at home, I took a job turning hamburgers at Walt's Patio Drive-In. This explanation didn't seem to matter to "Mr. B." He was brutal, as if his anger in having to support his love of coaching by teaching math on the side to ingrates like me was an injustice for which I should be punished. He took that anger and frustration out on me in class, where I became his "example" whenever I made a mistake in the homework or class work. My grade fell from a marginal A to a questionable B and, finally, lower. I tried as hard as I could, working to recapture the classroom magic. But as hard as I tried, I was always just below the "C" — just about correct. I came so close. I pleaded with "Mr. B." not to give me a D for the term, but he said, true to form, "Close only counts in horseshoes, hand grenades, and herpes."

From that year on I've hated math.

"Mr. B." made a lasting impression on me. Teachers have that power. It wasn't until the final quarter of my senior year in college — six years later — that I attempted another math course. Geometry was almost the end of the road in my math journey. The college course, basic math probabilities, reintroduced me to numbers just before the compulsory statistics course in graduate school. For six years, I viewed math as an enemy — something to be avoided at all costs.

On the brighter side, my aversion to math made me embrace the world of literature and language. After a brief dalliance with music, my other love, I found myself enthralled with the words, metaphors, and messages in English, Russian, and American literature. I found passion in reading and discussing great works; power in finding my voice through creative writing; logic in rhetoric and composition; magic in the written word. If "Mr. B." played a small role in influencing these discoveries, perhaps I can forgive him after all. Maybe he's not the evil presence I made him out to be.

He didn't ruin my life — but he came so close.

We each have the capacity to be "Mr./Ms. B." Our deliberate and our unintentional influences on students have the potential to send them in new, unexpected directions. "Mr. B." didn't set out to make me hate math (as far as I know), nor did he mysteriously intend for me to love words (I don't give him *that* much credit). Chances are he didn't care. He didn't even come close.

Someone else did.

He was ex-military, in his fifties, balding but with a startling white beard. "Mr. M." was the director of the university center at my undergraduate college. He ran a tight ship — the building was incredibly clean and well maintained, the staff was highly trained, and everything was expected to "work" — but this ship operated with a human touch, not an iron hand. "Mr. M." hired me late in my freshman year to work at the information desk in the center.

"Mr. M." expected total quality customer service, long before the idea became trendy. We were expected to leave no question unanswered, no student or staff member unsatisfied; we would follow the question to its logical conclusion. We were expected to dress professionally: shirts and ties for the men, dresses for the women (this was the early 1970s, after all). We were expected to treat everyone — from the custodial staff to the university's president to the campus visitor — with dignity and respect. "Even if you have to tell someone to go to hell," he once told me, "you need to make sure that they're going to enjoy the trip."

Within a year, "Mr. M." had promoted me to the Student Night Manager position. This was a momentous occasion, since I was the first non-vet to achieve this position under "Mr. M." He decided to take a chance on me. In this capacity, I learned to take responsibility for an entire building and all that happened within its walls, to feel like I owned the place, if only during my watch. I learned to see functions from the eyes of the user — the setup, the air conditioning, the overall appearance and "feel" of the room — and I learned to anticipate their needs and questions. I learned to listen. I met "Mr. M.'s" expectations.

On the side, I became involved in program board functions, working as part of the stage crew and crowd control. I attended Student Government Association meetings, ran for office (lost), and was appointed to create an off-campus housing referral office for SGA. The university center became my "real" home; the dormitories and apartments were just places to sleep.

One fall afternoon in my senior year, leaving the building after a full day of activities, "Mr. M." asked me an interesting question.

"Have you ever thought about working full-time in a university center?"

No, I hadn't thought about it. I didn't know there was such a thing as college student personnel administration. I'd come to college, first as a music major and later as an English major, thinking I'd probably become a high school teacher. "Mr. M." told me about the field and its opportunities and challenges. He mentioned the master of education program at a nearby college and suggested I look into it — if I was interested.

I was.

From that moment on, I knew I wanted to be the director of a university center. "Mr. M." introduced me to a world that I didn't know existed. His letter of reference (I still have a copy) helped open the door for an interview, and I was thrilled to be admitted into graduate school — something I would never have imagined back in "Mr. B.'s" class, when I wondered if I would even pass the tenth grade. I worked for "Mr. M." until the day I started my assistantship in graduate school.

I never asked him, but I assume that "Mr. M." had different ideas about coming close. Somehow, he saw in me potential and worth. As a mentor, he helped me acquire the skills, knowledge, and interest I needed to start the professional journey, which resulted in the career I love. As a model, he demonstrated that caring and compassion mixed with good management results in leadership. Other mentors and other models followed "Mr. M." — but he showed me a potential direction for my life.

We each have the capacity to be "Mr./Ms. B." or "Mr./Ms. M.," deliberately or unintentionally. Either way, we may not always be aware when we're influencing our students or pushing them in new, unexpected directions. We should strive to be more intentional in modeling for and mentoring our students — as did "Mr. M." — and diligently avoid actions or practices that marginalize our students — as did "Mr. B." Chances are we can show the way — or at least come close.

REFLECTION

1) Who are the Mr./Ms. B.'s and Mr./Ms. M.'s in your life? What lessons did you learn from each?

2) What role do you play in identifying and encouraging the next generation of professionals in your field?

3) In your work with students, particularly student leaders and employees, do you allow them to come close (horseshoes and hand grenades) or do you expect them to be right on target (bulls-eyes)? How do you handle their mistakes?

Working Without a Net

"I'm up on the tightwire

Flanked by life and the funeral pyre

Putting on a show for you to see."

LEON RUSSELL

AH, the circus. What a wonderful way to get away from the day-to-day trials and tribulations of higher education.

Every spring, a small, world-weary, traveling circus visits my small, untainted, immobile community. Every year, the canvas and rigging spread out across an open field of grass to be magically transformed into the big top. Every year, free tickets are doled out to school children to insure that parents will buy overpriced reserve seats, prepackaged cotton candy, stale popcorn, watery soft drinks, programs to be signed by the surly clowns, rides on bedraggled elephants, balloons with lifespans slightly shorter than the average housefly, and a broad assortment of other valuable souvenirs. Every year, I go with my youngest daughter — because it's what dads and daughters do.

I couldn't help but notice the last few times we've gone that the people selling tickets and programs, setting up the three rings, and ushering spectators to their seats are also the "artists" who tame the white tigers ... and complete daring acts of acrobatics ... and clown around between the attractions ... and fly through the air with the greatest of ease — through quick costume changes on the outskirts of the big top. The usher who helped us find our seat returned as an acrobat from Romania; later she was a trapeze artist from Mexico; finally, she emerged as a Bulgarian hula hoop performer. I suspect she was feeding the tigers while she was out of view. It was amazing how easily she changed her job description and her nationality.

We've all heard about people who wear several hats; in the circus world, the expression must be people who wear several *tights*.

———•———

The trapeze act has long been one of my favorites. Perhaps this fascination springs from the old song, "The Man on the Flying Trapeze." It could be scenes from old circus movies, like *The Greatest Show on Earth*. Or maybe it's simply the notion of swinging on a star. I love to see the grace, agility, and drama that play out above the silent spectators, who are holding their breath to see if the athletic young trapeze artist will actually complete a triple somersault and end up in the strong hands of his or her colleague.

This spring, I was disappointed.

First, the net should have been a dead giveaway (pardon the pun). The better the circus, the less likely that safety nets will be used. This circus had a large net suspended below the trapeze.

Second, one of the trapeze artists — the "catcher," for lack of the appropriate term — seemed to be out of shape. Don't get me wrong: if anyone needs to spend more time in the gym or on the trail, it's me. But this guy was huge. I caught myself hoping that the rigging holding up the trapeze equipment was well secured; it looked a little worse for the wear from where I sat.

Third, the "flyer" didn't seem to have the air of self-confidence that I've come to expect from trapeze artists. This guy looked worried: not a good sign.

The flyer, assisted by two women who were allegedly his sisters, made a few preliminary passes, then tried something a little more challenging: the triple somersault. The circus band stopped. The drum roll commenced. The flyer kicked off his platform, swung out toward the catcher once, twice, then let go of his trapeze on the third pass. For a few seconds, almost as if in slow motion, he twirled through open space close to the canvas near the top of the tent. As he began to descend, he reached out for his catcher.

And missed.

A few people screamed or gasped. The flyer fell to the net, bounced a few times, and then raised his hands to the audience. Polite applause.

He tried again.

And missed.

On his third attempt, he completed the somersault and succeeded in reaching the outstretched hands of his catcher. This time, the audience responded more enthusiastically.

It could all have been an act, but I don't think so. The look of frustration and disappointment on his face was too authentic. I think he failed, not through lack of skill but because of the net. I think he depended on the net to be there to catch him when he fell. He depended on the net more than he depended on his catcher, and more than he depended on himself. The safety net wasn't there to catch him; it was there to hold him back.

That's easy for me to say, of course. I've never attempted to hurl myself through the air, depending on skill, timing, and trust to keep me from falling to serious injury or death. The critic never takes the risk of the gladiator. Still, the episode made we wonder: do I work with a net or do I have self-reliance and an expectation that others will be there, be strong, and be trustworthy and trusting? If I know the net is there to catch me when I fall, am I more likely to fall? If the net is removed, am I more likely to reach out? The net is not the problem; safety and security are pretty wonderful concepts. But when we over-rely on the net, we keep ourselves from growing.

We could use several circus metaphors to describe our work in student affairs. To be successful, we must continually perform a balancing act. Much of what we do is as difficult as mating elephants (unless it's their idea). Every day we walk the tightrope, put up with clowns, and jump through hoops. We're frequently called upon to serve as ringmasters of our respective three-ring circuses.

To be successful, we too must wear several tights. We're ushers, carneys, lion tamers, acrobats, and trapeze artists in our own rights. We don't have to change our nationality at a moment's notice, but we've all learned the value of being multicultural. We don't have to take our show on the road, but we have to make sure our big top is ready for each new audience.

I used to work with a substantial safety net. It was called a university center. I grew increasingly comfortable knowing that the university center "net" was spread out all around me in the form of a great staff, an adequate budget, and a history of good programs and services. I made sure the net was appropriately secured and maintained by reinforcing the policies and procedures guiding our interactions. The net was tested from time to time by student activism, institutional politics, budget constraints, and competition from other departments, but it always held.

On most days, I never left the net to see what was happening in the other three rings of the campus. I began to see my net as the center ring — whatever was happening in the rest of the circus was of no concern to me. We had one of the best nets in our region, but our act was growing stale; we depended on the net to be there if we fell.

The more I focused on maintenance of the net and its inherent status quo, the less I focused on performance, achievement, and student needs. Our goals were written in the form of activities for staff, not outcomes for students. Student learning and student development — the very reasons the university center existed — were upstaged by our focus on image, amenities, comfort, and job security. Services were provided at the convenience of staff, not when students needed them. Enforcement of policy took precedence over interpretation of policy. The university center grew in physical size, number of personnel, scope of programs, and reputation, but I never stopped to see if the greatest show on earth was reaching the right audience. My part of the campus "big top" was clean, efficiently run, and a lot of fun; it had a safety net that couldn't be beat.

As director, I didn't think of the university center as a safety net. I was proud of the facilities, the staff, the programs and services, and the high esteem in which we were held by most of the campus. It wasn't until I advanced from that position and assumed new campuswide responsibilities that I began to understand something about my safety net: It wasn't there to catch me; it was there to hold me back.

I'm working without a net now, in a new job, without the physical and psychological trappings of a building or a department to call my own. I've been asked to create and influence relationships crossing divisional lines to achieve university-wide goals. I'm charged with facilitating interdisciplinary teams to integrate, create, and relocate programs and services in student success centers, breaking through some of the functional silos that permeate the contemporary university.

Without the safety of the net, I've rediscovered the value of spreading my wings. I'm reading books, attending conferences, and participating in training to develop skills and to acquire knowledge foreign to my professional preparation. I'm a born-again, lifelong learner. Beyond simply following the trends and issues of a rather narrowly defined discipline, I'm developing new attitudes and insights about the entire higher education enterprise. Like a skilled trapeze artist, I'm learning to reach out to my colleagues and to rely on their capabilities rather than an imaginary safety net. It's risky, but it's also exhilarating. This book is largely a result of my post-safety-net life.

From time to time we have to work without a net. It's great to learn from our mistakes, but if *all* we learn from our mistakes is that it's OK to make mistakes, we haven't really learned. We need to learn things we haven't learned, try things we've never tried, and take chances beyond our routines. We also need to learn that there are consequences associated with making mistakes — consequences for ourselves and for others. We have to get beyond the notion that we'll always have nets to catch us. If we don't, we'll never learn to reach out and grab the opportunities that lie just beyond our grasp. Until we lose our reliance on the net, we'll keep falling.

Higher education *is* in many ways the greatest show on earth. Step right up! Don a topcoat, a rubber nose, or a set of tights — and forget about the nets.

REFLECTION

1) What are some of the nets on which you rely? Do they help you or hinder you in your work?

2) Should our role in higher education be to provide safety nets for our students, or to teach the students so that they don't need nets?

3) What other circus metaphors (within this essay or from your own imagination) describe your current work situation? How could you use these metaphors as teaching or training tools?

Auto Biography

"We didn't know;

When there's plenty of gas,

There's no place to go..."

R.L.M.

Road Trip 1 (Plenty of Gas)

WHEN my brother left for the Army, I inherited the Magic Dustmobile, a mid-sized, heavy, black tank of a car built of steel and hope and rust. This '63 Plymouth Valiant was covered with an assortment of bumper stickers and had two qualities: a good heater and a clear radio with plenty of bass. Four bald tires somehow got me through my senior year of high school (I borrowed tires from a friend long enough to pass state inspection), and I, like so many of my generation, used the car for more than transportation. It was my home away from home, my ticket to independence, and a prerequisite to dating in my small hometown.

Long before the Colorado fields of corn and sugar beets became subdivision yards and split foyers, we cruised faster than reason and discretion — with the windows down — a million miles away from distant wars in the Far East, the sit-ins at coastal colleges, and a world changing faster than the speed we drove. Gas was 24 cents a gallon. No one dreamed of a fuel crisis: we trusted our cars to the men who wore those stars. We made promises we couldn't keep, plans we didn't understand, and scenarios impossible to realize.

We grew up in our cars. Behind the wheel we found the risk of adventure and romance. We had low Standards, but we were upwardly Mobil and coming out of our Shells.

After all, we had tigers in our tanks.

Looking back on those days is like driving into the sun with a dirty windshield: you can't see clearly through the glare. I sold the car for extra money when I left for college. Subsequent cars came and went, somewhat like the friendships and relationships that crowded my college and early adult years. The cars and friends and relationships became more instrumental and less magical over time. It wasn't that they stalled or broke down; they just became something on which to depend. We made promises we *could* keep, plans we *had to* understand, and scenarios impossible *not* to realize. We grew up, bought mini-vans, closed the power windows, and drove the speed limit listening to NPR. We checked under the hood for maintenance rather than excitement and wonder.

Our tanks were full, but our engines ran much cooler.

Somewhere down the line, I realized something I hadn't noticed in those high school days and nights, something that my generation would come to find in our rocky-road transition into adulthood.

When there's plenty of gas, there's no place to go.

Road Trip 2 (Two-lane Exit)

> *sometimes we drove each other crazy*
>
> *sometimes we took each other home*
>
> *we were just two travelers*
>
> *going it together, alone*

U.S. 85 veers off from I-76 eastbound about five miles northeast of Denver, and the plains spread out in three directions away from the purple mountains to the west, visible on those increasingly rare days when the smog doesn't smother the horizon. At this interchange, three lanes divide to become four: two lead eastward through the cattle and the corn to eventually cross over into Nebraska, while the other two head north through the sugar beets and potatoes to Wyoming.

> *sometimes we took the road for granted*
>
> *sometimes it took us for a ride*
>
> *we were just two passengers*
>
> *looking for the landmarks on the side*

It was that middle lane that fascinated me, separating abruptly to go both ways and making it possible for me to defer until the last possible moment my choice of direction. Even when my final destination was predetermined, I always drove in that middle lane, thinking there was the slightest chance that some impulse, some vision might make me choose the other way. It wasn't really a matter of Frost's "less-traveled road." It was the seduction of fate, the wonder of possibility, the "what if?"

sometimes we drove into the sunset

sometimes we couldn't start at all

we were just two messengers

looking for the writing on the wall

Shortly before the interchange, an obligatory large, green road sign with white lettering and arrows announced the possible destinations attached to a left or right turn. Beneath the sign, appearing as somewhat of an afterthought, was a smaller sign that said, "Two-lane Exit." The sign became a metaphor for me in my impressionable college years, and it has stuck with me through innumerable personal and professional decisions.

We have many two-lane exits in our lives and in our work. In much of what we do, there are elements of choice and chance. A colleague once remarked to me that we always have choices, even if we choose not to choose. Chance, sometimes called "fate," also plays its hand, but we still choose how we respond to chance. We can choose to take chances, or we can choose to *not* take chances and leave our choices to chance.

sometimes we filled it up completely

sometimes we let it all run dry

we were just two fugitives

on the run and never knowing why

At some point, each of us will play the various roles portrayed by the images in the lyrics from my song: traveler, passenger, messenger, or fugitive. These images suggest that we have varying degrees of control over the circumstances in our lives and our work. Regardless of the role we're playing, we can approach our metaphoric two-lane exits as foregone conclusions (*I have no choice in which way I must go…*), uninvited alternatives (*I'm forced to choose…*), or expanding opportunities (*I have the power to choose…*). Chances are, we choose the way we respond.

Road Trip 3 (Pay Attention)

To overstate the obvious, there are substantial differences between driving I-80 across the plains of Nebraska and taking I-70 over the mountains of Colorado. I-80 is about as close as a highway can come to the straight line between points A and B. The view from one exit to the next is interchangeable. In contrast,

I-70 winds up and down, left and right through the foothills and alpine terrain, rising more than 5,000 feet from the Front Range to the summit. The view is spectacular.

When you're driving any stretch of I-80, it's easy to relax, settle back into the seat, switch on the cruise control — maybe close just one eye. With an unchanging horizon in all directions and a straight and narrow path ahead, it's easy to be lulled into complacency and lethargy. There's beauty in the prairie, but the blacktop generally avoids it. Driving across Nebraska on I-80, it's all too easy to be lulled to sleep. The consequences can be disastrous. You try to keep your eyes on the road and the pedal to the metal, but sometimes you feel like a hawk flying into the wind, beating your wings furiously yet appearing to stay in one place.

In contrast, you have to pay attention when you're traversing the mountains on I-70. You can't take the road for granted. You have to be attuned to changing conditions. Around each corner, over each rise, lie endless surprises, endless challenges, and endless possibilities. You have to be awake to drive this highway. You're treated to some of the most outstanding vistas you'll ever see from an interstate road. Because you're forced to pay attention, you see even more than you might encounter under other driving circumstances.

Some people are content to drive highways like I-80. Unless the weather turns bad, you can make great gas mileage. No surprises. Some people feel they have no other options; they drive where they must. No choices. And some people prefer to drive highways like I-70; it's hard work, but the payoff is worth it. No regrets.

Road Trip 4 (Round Trip)

Many people in higher education long for simpler times.

They prefer those "good old days," when they knew what to expect. They could plan ahead and be reasonably assured that nothing would interrupt those plans. The tried-and-true stayed true no matter how many times they tried it. Change was something they carried in their pockets, not something that carried them. Their I-80 days were comfortable, predictable, manageable. They had plenty of gas in their tanks, even though there was no particular place to go. Unlimited resources didn't necessarily translate into better programs, better services, better ideas, or better education for their students. Nonetheless, they had a nice, comfortable ride.

We're now in I-70 days. There are curves and hills in our paths, and they demand our attention. We can't drive with one eye closed and depend on cruise control. We've got to have both hands on the wheel, continually assessing and adjusting to the changing road conditions of our profession. But because we're paying attention, we'll see things we've never seen before. New opportunities. New visions. New answers to old questions. New paths to undiscovered destinations. Perhaps the changing environment and limited resources will bring out the best in us — if we're paying attention.

REFLECTION

1) Is your organization currently experiencing I-80 conditions or I-70 conditions?

2) If you "checked under the hood" of your organization, what would you find? As you did your checking, what would you have in mind: maintenance, or excitement and wonder?

3) What two-lane exits (choices) are you currently facing, personally or in your organization? In this regard, do you feel you're a traveler, a passenger, a messenger, or a fugitive — that is, how much control of the circumstances do you feel you have, and how is this affecting your choices?

The Definite Article

"Them and us, them and us

Ashes to ashes, dust to dust."

DON HENLEY AND DANNY KORTCHMAR

I'VE noticed something about the word "the." Maybe you have, too.

Whenever I hear it preceding a group of people — as in *the* faculty or *the* administration or *the* Greeks or *the* black students or *the* athletes — I get ready for the stereotype that follows.

The implication here is that everyone who gets corralled under this label is the same.

The faculty. I know a good number of faculty members, and I haven't found two yet who are alike. Not even close. They each have different backgrounds, different approaches to their discipline and subject matter, different skills and methods, different personalities, and different ways of looking at the world. How can I possibly say the faculty and have it mean something (nudge nudge, wink wink, know what I mean, say no more)? That's how we label people.

The administration. After twenty years in the profession, I'm still not quite sure what this word means or who it includes. Does it mean the president and his or her immediate staff? The vice presidents? The deans, directors, and department heads? The associate and assistant directors of various programs, functions, and departments? The program advisors and coordinators? Just who is the administration? Many students, faculty, and staff use this term as if they know, but I have yet to hear their answer. Maybe they don't know either. Maybe it's simply how we label people.

The Greeks. Now there's an easy target (and I'm guilty of this one myself). Regardless of *the* student enrollment, diversity in Greek organizations, varying levels of involvement in service, and varying degrees of academic success accomplished by chapters, we collapse a frequently significant proportion of *the* campus into this expression. That's how we label people.

The black students (substitute any race or ethnicity you choose). They're all a part of *the* same group, so that must mean they all think, feel, learn, act, and react similarly, right? Wrong. That's how we label people.

The athletes. Another easy target. Despite *the* varying educational capabilities, personal interests, and personal motivations of our student-athletes, we cast collective aspersions on them simply because they are athletes and therefore not serious students. That's how we label people.

When we label people this way, we disallow any notion of individuality. Every person is expected to fit *the* stereotypes, paradigms, and preconceived notions, as well as all of *the* expectations we define and hold for people whom we put into that category. We're not required to think in terms of our relationship with that individual — just in terms of *the* characterization we've created.

Working with student government for several years, I experienced *the* labeling on a weekly basis that came so easily to many student leaders (I could have written *the* student leaders here, but I caught myself in time). "*The* multicultural groups want too much money." (*Which groups aren't multicultural?*) "*The* administration won't support *the* faculty on this." (*Which administrators and which faculty?*) "*The* Republicans don't understand compassion." "*The* Democrats don't understand responsibility." (*Let's divide the world into camps, why don't we.*) "*The* newspaper staff is out to get us." (*God bless collegiate Woodwards and Bernsteins*). Student government, faculty senate, and other similar bodies have often mastered *the* utilization of *the* definite article and *the* collective noun.

The definite article.

The, as far as I can tell, means one.

Although we have one faculty, we have numerous faculty members teaching in numerous departments under several college designations. Although we have one administration, we have numerous higher education professionals working on administrative tasks. We don't have one set of Greeks or minority students or students with special interests; we have hundreds and thousands of students with diverse needs, interests, and abilities. Unless we're talking about one individual, there's no such thing as *the*.

Why do we use these labels? Maybe we're lazy. It's easy to categorize people into common sets instead of trying to see *the* multiple connections, influences, inspirations, motivations, and constraints that define *the* individual. Maybe we're prejudiced. Much of what we're taught in our homes, schools, and self-selected organizations forces us to differentiate people as "like me" or "unlike me," "right" or "wrong," "safe" or "unsafe," "saved" or "damned," "us" or "them."

Labels on food products can't come close to approximating the flavor, texture, or aroma of the product itself. Similarly, labels on people don't work either. Prejudging an individual based on labels is like eating only the labels of food products; you won't know what you've really got, you'll never be satisfied, and you'll be left with a bad taste in your mouth.

An alternative? Drop *the*. Assume you can't put everyone into convenient sets. Challenge people when they stereotype others. Model nonjudgmental behavior.

Think in terms of relationships between individuals rather than between groups. Assume that everything you learned isn't necessarily true. Test your prejudices in real life and in real time.

Whenever *the* comes up in written or verbal communication — even in thought — see if you can substitute something other than a definite article (*e.g.*, "some"). Avoid absolutes (absolutely).

It's unlikely that any group agrees on everything all of *the* time. Beyond trying to condense complex issues into simple equations, let's be aware of and examine — and hopefully learn to appreciate — differences, ambiguity, complexity, and *the* fact that we don't have all of *the* answers.

REFLECTION

1) What are some additional examples of labels we use to categorize groups of people, and what are the bases of these labels?

2) How would you use the notion of labeling, definite articles, collective nouns, etc., to assist a student or a group of students in overcoming their prejudices? What about staff?

3) What labels does your organization tend to use in dealing with its constituents? What can you do to change that?

Private Holidays

"You're a holiday
Every day, such a holiday."

BARRY AND ROBIN GIBB

IT comes once a year, generally in early to mid September. There aren't any greeting cards to commemorate the day. Business establishments don't alter their schedules, and postal employees still make their appointed rounds. It's a day that's not on your calendar. Actually, no one knows about this holiday except for my family, a few close friends, and me.

It's called Salsa Saturday.

How do you celebrate Salsa Saturday? And well you might ask! First, make sure you pick a day free of any other distractions. Chores or diversions can't interrupt Salsa Saturday. Next, get up at dawn and go to the nearest farmers' market to select a couple of bushels of tomatoes, a variety of sweet and hot peppers, and some onions. Pick out a dozen roses or a bouquet of fresh flowers. Just because.

Take the ingredients home. Before retreating to the kitchen, select some music — preferably something you know well. Play it loud enough so your singing doesn't bother the other residents.

Don a favorite apron. Mine is a custom job with the inscription: "Mitchell's Hot Sauce: It'll burn you a new one!" Have rubber gloves on hand (pardon the pun) for slicing the hot stuff.

If you're lucky, you have an apparatus that crushes tomatoes and pushes the seeds and skin out one opening and the "meat" out another, preventing a lot of time spent slicing and peeling the fruit. A food processor for the peppers is helpful, but I prefer the hand-diced approach when I have time.

Cook the tomatoes down. Way down. For the consistency you want, it takes about five or six hours. Along the way, add the fresh peppers and onions, a touch of cilantro, some dried crushed peppers, a little lime juice, and salt. Put on another tape or CD: you're going to be here all day.

In the early evening, the canning process begins. By now the entire house smells like a Mexican restaurant. Carefully scoop and pour the salsa into jars: pints and half-pints are best. Can until you drop — then sample.

Just because.

I can't imagine fall without Salsa Saturday. It's one way I celebrate the harvest, the passing of summer and the coming of fall. It's a private holiday.

In a short visit to Paris, my first trip abroad, I learned that it's possible to celebrate living every day. It doesn't take a national holiday or a momentous occasion. Today is reason enough. A breakfast of fresh bread and cheese, an afternoon in the park, an evening sampling wine and exotic dishes, a late-night walk along the Seine — each act is a celebration conducted by hundreds of thousands of people on a daily basis. Parisians seem to understand this. Americans seem to be too busy being too busy.

Though not quite as exquisite, we have our own versions of fresh bread and cheese in America. Parks are generally within reach, and some of our campuses are parks in their own right. Evening offers many opportunities for repast and reflection. If we tried, we could reclaim the night. We have plenty of reasons to celebrate living: we could have more.

The simple art of enjoying today is all too often lost in the struggle for a better tomorrow. But here's the catch: tomorrow will be just like today unless we change today.

Maybe we should be working today to make a better yesterday tomorrow. Think about it.

If you truly believe that your work in student affairs or higher education is important — that your efforts have a positive impact on your students and their world — then you have cause to celebrate. If you look at the first day of each semester or term the same way you view New Year's Day — as a day of hope and new beginnings — then you have cause to celebrate. If you wake up most days with the attitude that you *get* to go to work today — that the day will be filled with surprises, insights, and inspiration — then you have cause to celebrate. If you feel a personal sense of pride when you watch your student volunteers or employees wear their caps and gowns — graduating with new skills, knowledge, and perspectives desperately needed in a changing world — then you have cause to celebrate. If you feel at the end of the day that you've done your best — that you learned from your mistakes, profited from your experiences, and gave it the old college try — then you have cause to celebrate.

Private holidays. If you could, what would you celebrate? Every day a new year begins. Every day is a day to champion civil rights. Every day is a day in which you can fall in love. Every day we're resurrected. Every day is a day to honor a mother or a father. Every day we have the opportunity to celebrate our independence and our interdependence. Every day is filled with potential tricks and treats. Every day offers something for which to be thankful. Every day miraculous births take place. Every night is a holy night. Every day could have been your birthday. Every day is an anniversary.

Private holidays can happen at work, at home, on the road, or wherever you happen to be. What's more, private holidays ought to be celebrated in the midst of our other activities. Celebrate the support you receive from colleagues, and give them cause to celebrate by being the type of colleague you'd want them to be. Celebrate the appreciation you receive from students, and give them cause to celebrate by sharing with them your joy for learning and development. Celebrate the love you receive from family and friends, and give them cause to celebrate by making each day a celebration of life and love. Celebrate just because.

Have a private holiday.

REFLECTION

1) If you could create a national holiday, what would you celebrate?

2) Are you too busy being too busy to enjoy what you're doing today? (Be honest!) What can you do to change that?

3) What potential private holidays could you celebrate?
   What private holidays might your organization observe?

Leadership Recipes

"A lot of bread and gangs of meat,

Oodles of butter and something sweet,

Gallons of coffee to wash it down,

And bicarbonate of soda by the pound ..."

CHARLES E. CALHOUN

I'D like to share some of my recipes with you. To be honest, they aren't all original recipes, but that's one of the nice things about recipes: they're made for sharing. I've borrowed a few ingredients here, added a few secrets there, and hopefully come up with something you'll find nourishing. You'll probably be relieved to know that I'm somewhat of a short-order cook, not a chef; these recipes are intended to satisfy your appetite, not provide you with a balanced meal. You're responsible for your own diet.

I've worked with leadership programs for years, but my earliest professional experience — using the term quite loosely — was as a teenage chef in a large restaurant. I've subsequently tried to find a way to synthesize these two areas of experience into what I've come to call "Leadership Recipes."

I started working in restaurants when I was thirteen years old. In a twelve-month period, I went from busboy to dishwasher to cook's helper to fry cook and, ultimately, to full-fledged cook, with no formal preparation. The Del Camino was a major complex that included a banquet facility, a coffee shop, two gas stations, a truck stop, a lounge with live entertainment, and a convenience store. The opportunities were as plentiful as were the turnover and the grease.

Although I ultimately discovered that I wasn't really suited for a life in food service, I did learn a lot about food service, business, and life in general. And in this setting, I began to learn about leadership as well.

Shel Silverstein, one of my favorite poets, offers a recipe for a hippo sandwich in one of his poems, "Recipe for a Hippo Sandwich" (which appears in *Where the Sidewalk Ends*). After describing the necessary ingredients — bread, mayonnaise, onion, hippo, pepper, etc. — he tells us that making the sandwich is easy. The problem is biting into it.

That seems to be the problem with leadership: biting into it. The word leadership has been kicked around quite a lot in government, business, education, religion, and just about every other facet of our lives. We all know we need it, we recognize it when we see it, but we don't always know how to translate it to others.

We spend a great deal of time on our campuses creating and conducting programs to help develop the inherent leadership in our students. The responsibility of education, as we see it, is not merely to pass on knowledge or information. We also need to help people become better citizens, better contributors to society, better employees, better managers, better spouses and partners, better parents — in short, better leaders. And the leadership we're talking about doesn't necessarily mean the type associated with hero worship or legendary figures. We're talking about leadership as a shared social responsibility.

We're also talking about what James McGregor Burns (in his 1992 address to the Jepson Leadership School Summer Institute) defined as "transforming leadership," and what Steven Covey defined as "principle-centered leadership" (in his 1991 book of the same title). Transforming leadership focuses on how to make things better and how to add to people's accomplishments, contrasted with the traditional form of "transactional leadership," in which we attempt to buy the loyalty of supporters through rewards and consequences. Principle-centered leadership focuses on the time-tested, universal principles that should be at the heart of every action we take or decision we make. Principles transcend personal or group values, and these principles can be found at the heart of major world religions. To be a principle-centered leader, according to Covey, is to be a light and a model, not a judge or a critic.

In effect, principle-centered, transforming leadership should be our goal. But I'm going to approach it using a different metaphor, perhaps one with which we can all identify.

In all groups and organizations, someone is selected, elected, or hired to be the leader. Certainly each of us fits into this scenario somewhere. You have probably noticed that there's a difference between being selected the leader and actually leading. Unfortunately, we have far more bosses than leaders, and bosses are much more likely to impose change rather than inspire it. Holding a position of authority, gaining experience, having the desire to lead — none of these conditions automatically translates into leadership. Leadership requires developing a combination of knowledge, skills, and competencies, and appropriately employing these ingredients in response to — or in anticipation of — circumstances.

Rick Miller, a prolific presenter and author on leadership topics, created "The Elixir of Leadership" back in 1987 (see *Campus Activities Programming* magazine, Vol. 20, No. 2). His elixir included several primary ingredients: communication, motivation, action, perseverance, honesty, care, risk, resourcefulness, and creativity. I've borrowed liberally from his ingredients, but I'm the kind of cook who can't leave well enough alone; I've customized his ingredients to my own tastes.

As a leader, you're the head chef of your group. You need to combine the right ingredients in just the right way to come up with the right flavor, adding your own secret spices as necessary. Given the right ingredients, what might we cook up? Let's just see.

Communication is an essential ingredient in leadership. Effective leaders must, in the words of my youngest daughter, "listen very loud." How you say what you say, how you use symbols and metaphors, how you employ body language and cultural expressions — all of these factors communicate right along with the words themselves. If the kitchen staff can't communicate, the entrées and appetizers and desserts will never make it out of the kitchen.

Encouragement is an essential ingredient in leadership. Motivation must always come from inside. It's impossible to motivate others: you can only trigger their motivation. A favorite poster of mine states, "If your ship doesn't come in, swim out to it." The chef understands the difference between offering the kitchen staff choices and chances rather than duties and burdens. Choices and chances are incentives; duties and burdens are obstacles. Encouragement for success is much more powerful than threats for failure.

Performance is an essential ingredient in leadership. Garth Brooks sings in his song, "The River," "I'll never reach my destination if I never try." If the hardest part of any project is starting, you as the leader must set the rolling pin rolling. With your sleeves rolled up and your apron on, you'll be sending a message to the rest of the kitchen: *We can do it, and I'll do it with you!*

Determination is an essential ingredient in leadership. Walter Elliot suggested that perseverance is a series of short races, not a long race. You reach your destinations through single steps; you accomplish your goals by incremental tasks and projects. Like Ulysses S. Grant, it's possible to lose your way to victory. After numerous failures, Thomas Edison replied, "Well, I've found several hundred things that don't work. I'm on my way. Triumph may be around the corner." Only the cook who tries and fails and tries again will discover new tastes and textures.

Integrity is an essential ingredient in leadership. I once heard a story about a suspicious baker who wondered if the pounds of butter he bought from a neighboring farmer were accurate proportions. He weighed the butter on his scale and, sure enough, found that he was getting less than he was paying for. The farmer was arrested, and the judge discovered that the farmer had no scales. Dismayed, he asked the farmer how he could measure the butter without scales. "It's easy, your honor," replied the farmer. "I buy a one-pound loaf of bread from the baker and measure my butter against his bread." (See *Wellsprings of Wisdom* by R.L. Woods, 1969, page 34.) Modeling leadership behavior means you're both trusting and trustworthy.

Humor is an essential ingredient in leadership. Humorist Charles Lindner once said: "A person has two legs and one sense of humor, and if you're faced with the choice, it's better to lose a leg." This may be a bit extreme, but being able to laugh at your own mistakes will show your kitchen staff, especially new members, that you're human. Humor has recently emerged as an important training tool in health care, education, and business; attention is being given to the healing qualities of humor. The shelves of our leadership kitchen should be well stocked with it.

Caring is an essential ingredient in leadership. There's no such thing as a leader who doesn't care. You can't be a leader and not care about your people, about process, about the community, about the world. Caring and competence are an incredible combination. It's this combination that distinguishes a leader from a manager. If you care to lead, you need to lead with care. With care in the kitchen, every banquet will be memorable.

Risk taking is an essential ingredient in leadership. The kitchen staff must have confidence in themselves, competence in specific tasks, and reasonable chances to succeed. They need to take risks in order to gain confidence and competence. Part of risk taking is the risk the leader takes in trusting others. By modeling trust and by being trustworthy, the leader demonstrates to the followers that risk taking is a valuable and rewarding experience. I understand that somewhere there is a group known as the Giraffe Society that honors people who stick their necks out and defy the spread of mediocrity and indifference. I'd have to say that leaders are more likely to be giraffes than, say, ostriches. Your job as chef is to help the kitchen staff achieve the appropriate level of risk taking.

Resourcefulness is an essential ingredient in leadership. Resourcefulness doesn't mean that you're full of resources; it means you're capable of making full use of the resources you have. People with unlimited resources aren't required to be resourceful. In an age of limited resources, you need to make sure that the members of your kitchen staff develop and use their own resourcefulness. Being resourceful means being good stewards of the resources with which we're entrusted — having an intrinsic abundance mentality in the face of extrinsic scarcity.

Creativity is an essential ingredient in leadership. Creativity, from a leadership standpoint, is the ability to imagine and then engineer ideas into reality. Call it "imagineering," for lack of a better term. Leaders must maintain a piece of childhood, a taste of the artist, and a continuing sense of wonder and magic. Leaders involve others in creatively solving problems, generating new ideas, and brainstorming ideas into life. Add creativity for flavor whenever the menu starts getting bland.

After completely blending all of these ingredients, you, as the chef, need to light a fire under the mixture, stirring until the mixture comes to a slow boil. Now, you serve. And service is probably the most important word I can think of when it comes to leadership. That one word exemplifies leadership. Everything you do as a leader should be intended to serve the organization, just as your organization's purpose should be to serve the larger community in some way. To lead, you must serve. Your organization is your kitchen; the dining room is the community. In the final analysis, your efforts result in the banquet of success and achievement.

I love to cook, but not for money. Breakfast is my specialty. Give me an uncommitted Saturday or Sunday morning, a good gas stove, cast iron cookware, fresh eggs and fruit, a well-stocked pantry, a cappuccino maker to the side, and some good music on the stereo and I'll give you a breakfast you won't forget.

When I cook, I think of the recipe as a suggestion, not a requirement — an opportunity, not an obligation. To perform with food, you have to improvise. If the recipe calls for two cups of milk, I might substitute a cup of flavored yogurt one day, cottage cheese or sour cream another. What would happen if I added a can of mushroom soup to this casserole? How about a subtle hint of cinnamon? Maybe salsa would add a little zip. Why not lemon juice instead of vinegar?

Most of the time it works.

The same is true with leadership. If the only utensil in your kitchen were a knife, you'd begin to see every ingredient or mixture as something to be cut. But because you also have spoons, forks, ladles, mashers, mixers, blenders, etc., your opportunities for creative cuisine are enhanced. The recipe may be tried and true, but it's only the baseline. Experimentation and innovation add excitement, new flavors, new textures, and new opportunities.

I have a relative, bless her heart, who has one favorite menu that she always prepares for company. Always. It's not a bad meal, and she works hard to make everything come out great, but it's the same damn meal every time. The first few times I had this meal, I was satisfied. Later, I was amused. Now, I look for excuses to avoid dining with her. It's nutritious, colorful, and balanced, but it's the same damn meal every time. Even my kids notice it. She's got the recipe down pat — she could probably make the meal by memory with her eyes closed if she so chose. While I can appreciate her effort, my idea of entertaining involves more creativity.

The practice of leadership can easily be perceived as that one special meal prepared over and over again for company. First, we're satisfied. Later, we're amused. Finally, we avoid the experience if we can. Leadership has to be creative. It has to involve taking risks. It has to inspire. It has to transform, not merely transact. It ought to be resourceful and fun. Recipes are suggestions, not requirements.

One last point. In a recent workshop on collaboration, a group of colleagues and I were attempting to identify some of the barriers to collaboration. One person mentioned how she often approached colleagues to create partnerships on projects or problems, only to be turned down because the other person had "too much on their plate." I wondered, out loud, if it was really a matter of having too much on their plate, or more a concern of not having the right things on their plate. A full plate can consist of a balanced meal; it can also be filled with condiments or desserts.

Effective leadership exhibits balance. When people tell you their plates are full, help them find a way to balance their diets. Share some of the tools and techniques you've developed to manage your time and priorities. Talk about workshops, articles, books, planners, time management systems — anything that helped you get control of your life. Share your recipes for leadership and success — and keep adding to your own cookbook by borrowing new recipes from your fellow diners in the higher education banquet.

REFLECTION

1) Do you have a recipe for leadership? What are the most important ingredients in your recipe, and why?

2) How flexible are your recipes? Do you follow the list or do you improvise?

3) What's on your plate? Do you have a balanced diet?

A New Coat of Paint

"Someday, everything is gonna be different
When I paint my masterpiece ..."

BOB DYLAN

I'M one of those crazy people who actually enjoys painting. I'm not talking about still life on canvas, and I don't do nudes. But give me an empty room, a good roller with a medium nap (the thickness of the fibers, not the rest you take between coats...), a two-inch tapered brush, some good tunes on the radio, a quality latex paint, and a dependable bucket and I'll give you a clean, fresh, semi-gloss finish.

Most of the people I know hate to paint. Some would rather visit the dentist than pick up the brush. Others prefer being audited. Not me. I like painting a room because it contrasts with my professional activity.

With painting, I clearly see what needs to be done. I can generally remove all of the distractions or obstacles before I begin. Good resources are easily accessible. I have to do some thinking about the work while I work, but not a great deal. My mind gets to go on vacation for a little while. If I make a mistake, I can usually paint over it. I see my progress. When I complete the job, I have visible confirmation of what I've done — and the room generally looks better than it did when I started.

When I'm finished, I'm finished.

Mowing the lawn offers similar benefits. I hated mowing the lawn when I was a kid. Now, it's actually a nice diversion. I can clearly see what needs to be done, especially if the dandelions have broken through. I can generally remove all of the distractions and obstacles before I begin, weather permitting. Good resources are easily accessible, particularly if I've taken care of mower maintenance in the spring. I have to do some thinking about the work while I work, but not a great deal. My mind gets to go on another vacation. It's hard to make a mistake mowing, and I can see my progress with each successive row I mow. When I complete the job, the lawn generally looks better than it did when I started.

When I'm finished, I'm finished.

Our professional activity isn't much like painting or mowing. We can't always clearly see what needs to be done: we have to use our intuition, instincts, professional judgment, training, and knowledge. We can't always remove all of the distractions and obstacles before we begin: our abilities to react, adjust, and change direction are critical in facing the unexpected circumstances that come our way. We don't always have the resources we need: creativity, resourcefulness, a little ingenuity, and a knack for cooperative collaboration are characteristics we have to possess to be successful. We have to keep thinking about the work while we work: mental vacations are a luxury we cannot afford. If we make a mistake, we can't simply paint over it: as much as we talk about learning from our mistakes, there are generally consequences that we can't ignore. We don't always see progress. When we finish a task or project, we rarely have visible confirmation of what we've done.

And when we're finished, we've just begun.

Don't get me wrong. I love my work (most of the time). My work requires problem solving, decision making, and creative energy. If it didn't, I'm not sure I'd be interested. Uncertainty, constant change, delayed gratification — these aren't for everyone, but they come with this particular piece of territory. That's why I find satisfaction in the contrast of physical activities unrelated to my professional work. I suppose that if my work was more routine, repetitive, and concrete, I'd have to find outside diversions that were more unpredictable, random, and abstract.

Contrasts like these help keep us in balance.

I used to love see-saw "surfing" when I was a child. This activity required a sense of balance and a general disregard for skinned knees and hands. I would gingerly walk up the see-saw board until I reached its fulcrum. As I stepped slightly forward, arms outstretched, the board would begin to level. By adjusting my weight, I could keep the board approximately horizontal. To stay "up" on my makeshift surfboard, I had to periodically make adjustments to my stance. The little lesson I learned in this activity was simply that balance isn't achieved by standing still; balance requires adjustments.

To achieve balance in our work and in our lives, we too must make periodic adjustments. Finding personal activities that contrast with our professional activities is one such adjustment. Balancing work and play is another important adjustment, as is balancing physical activity and mental activity.

Painting a wall or mowing the lawn may not be everyone's balancing act, but it works for me. What works for you?

REFLECTION

1) In what activities do you find contrast to your professional work? How do these activities help keep you balanced?

2) Which parts of your work have clearcut beginnings and endings? Which parts have neither? Do you prefer the parts with clearcut beginnings and endings or the parts that have neither? Why?

3) Does your job have enough stability? Enough creativity? If your job is lacking stability or creativity, how do you compensate for the imbalance?

Can't You Just Imagine?

"You may say I'm a dreamer
But I'm not the only one ..."

JOHN LENNON

AS far as I'm concerned, there's no vacation quite as restful and rejuvenating as a week at the beach. A week in a mountain cabin comes close, but the beach seems to bring out the best in our family.

For us, the beach is an eight-hour drive away. There are closer beaches — Virginia Beach is just down the road, and the Outer Banks of North Carolina are just beyond that — but we prefer Sunset Beach at the southernmost tip of North Carolina. People always ask where Sunset Beach is located when we tell them of our vacation destination; that's one reason we love it.

Over the drawbridge and across the causeway lies a pollution-free, traffic-free, commerce-free strand of beach houses, sand, and waves. Each year, when we reach the end of the causeway and see the first whitecaps of the waves, I can feel the tension slipping from my shoulders. I can smell the sea breeze and taste the salty air. I can see the looks of joy and contentment on my family members' faces — and on my own if I glance in the rearview mirror for a second.

Our favorite house, *Trader Jim's* by name, isn't quite on the beachfront, although for several years we had an unobstructed view. A pair of houses recently impinged on the vista that we once enjoyed from the screened porch and the rooftop deck. Still, *Trader Jim's* is an old friend. We *know* we're at the beach when our van, laden with bikes and floats and beach paraphernalia, pulls into the carport beneath the house. The house has just the right arrangement, just the right number of rooms, and it's just the right distance from the pier that serves as the destination for our evening walks. It's not a time-share, but it's there when we need it. Generally, by the first week in August we need it.

Once we put away the keys, the watches, the shoes, and all of the other trappings of civilization as we know it, we begin our daily regimen. A walk at dawn on the beach. Do-it-yourself breakfast on the front porch. Down to the beach to set up camp by mid-morning. Lunch on the beach or back at the house. An afternoon nap. Dinner of fresh shrimp (very fresh!) or a trip to a local seafood restaurant. An after-dark walk on the beach, perhaps to watch the sea turtles hatch or just to see the phosphorus glow beneath our feet. If we're still up for it, a game of cards or dominos ends the day. Sound boring? Just try it for a week and you'll see what I mean.

On such a week last summer, my youngest daughter and I were stargazing on the roof of the beach house. Above us, a sky much wider and darker than our "domestic" sky was filled with an amazing array of stars and constellations. To the west, a storm in the distance threatened the mainland with periodic lightning and whispers of thunder, but the sky to the east and south was clear. Lindsey and I talked about the day, about the grandparents who'd come to share the week with us, and about everything and nothing in particular. I asked her, "What if all of the stars were different colors, just like the strings of Christmas tree lights we use at home?" That question led to a string of other "what ifs." And those "what ifs" led to a song:

> *What if stars on summer nights*
>
> *were colored just like Christmas lights*
>
> *and planets could be flown like kites;*
>
> *can't you just imagine?*

On the way home from the beach, with grandparents deposited at the airport and the rest of the family sleeping in the van, Lindsey transcribed as I recaptured some of our ideas in verses for the song:

> *Wouldn't people be impressed*
>
> *if rainbows came at your request*
>
> *and filled the sky from east to west;*
>
> *can't you just imagine?*

John Lennon, in one of his signature songs, asked us to imagine some of the "big things," like religion, government, economic systems, war, and peace. There's nothing wrong with that kind of imagination: we need dreamers like Mr. Lennon. But Lindsey and I imagined some smaller things in our rooftop repartee:

> *Wouldn't it be kind of grand*
>
> *if ocean waves at your command*
>
> *could write your name across the sand;*
>
> *can't you just imagine?*

It wasn't that we really wanted these things to happen: imagination was the means and the end to our dreaming. It was one of the easiest, least expensive, most satisfying things to do at the beach, in the night, on the roof:

> *Imagination isn't hard and doesn't take much training;*
>
> *it often leads to new ideas, much faster than complaining.*
>
> *And even if the thoughts you think don't lead to new inventions,*
>
> *you had some fun along the way, along with good intentions.*

When Lindsey finished transcribing and joined her sisters and mother in back-seat slumber, I had a few quiet moments to reflect on imagination. Creativity, innovation, imagination — we seem to honor these notions, but we also seem to fear them. People with imagination are sometimes seen as non-conformists, less than realistic, given to flights of fancy, *dreamers*. Creativity isn't always practical, nor does it honor tradition and "common sense." Innovation means change, and change is challenge with the "ell" scared out of it (work with me on this one...):

> *Wouldn't it beat everything*
>
> *if you could teach the wind to sing*
>
> *an opera to start the spring;*
>
> *can't you just imagine?*

Yes, imagination sometimes gets us into trouble. It also has the potential to get us out of trouble:

> *What if people everywhere*
>
> *had different eyes and skin and hair*
>
> *and no one really seemed to care;*
>
> *can't you just imagine?*

My musical mentor (who just happened to be my educational mentor as well) taught me something about ideas. Beyond serving as my academic advisor, Norm was also the leader of the jazz trio with which I performed in college. He was twenty years my senior, an accomplished English professor and logician, not to mention an accomplished pianist. I learned more from him on the stage and in the car on our way to gigs than I did in his classroom, proving Astin's theory about involvement with faculty outside the classroom — at least in my case.

I was struggling to match the amazing solos created and performed by some of our fellow musicians. They played so effortlessly, hitting the right notes, capturing the right emotions, making music. Why couldn't I do that? I knew all of the scales. I'd studied music theory. I had technique. I had the best effects money could buy, from wah-wah pedals to phase shifters to reverb. Why didn't my solos sound like those I heard from other musicians?

Norm answered my question one evening during a long drive back from a four-hour gig in Scotts Bluff, Nebraska. It wasn't the effects pedals or even the guitar that made the solo, he told me. It wasn't how fast I could play thirty-second notes or how many chromatic scales I knew. It all came down to ideas. You had to have an idea about what you wanted to say in the solo. You had to understand that the silence or pause surrounding a note is just as important as the note. You had to understand that different volume levels communicate passion, understanding, warmth, power. You had to understand that before you played a single note, you had to have an idea. Good musicians have good ideas. Mediocre musicians have technique. Poor musicians try to cover their lack of ideas with technology.

I had no idea!

———•◦•———

Imagination matters in our work in student affairs and higher education. It isn't hard, and it doesn't take much training, contrary to the notion that only artists and fools have imagination. All children have imagination; it comes to life in their play. What would happen if we let our dormant imagination come out to play? Why do we have to hire consultants to teach us how to be creative? Worse yet, why do we hire people to *do* our creativity for us?

What if we redirected all of the energy we currently spend on lamenting our circumstances and complaining about the decisions affecting us toward playing the "what if" game? What if we tried something different? What if we asked others for their ideas? What if we were to start this organization from scratch: how would it be different? What if we trusted the people around us rather than assuming the worst, being surprised when the worst doesn't happen, and being affirmed when something does go wrong? What if we focused on ideas rather than technique and technology?

Can't you just imagine?

———•◦•———

Our song wasn't quite finished. I wrote a letter to my father, explaining the week at the beach to him and the pleasure I found in focusing on the family for an entire week. I also told him about the song Lindsey and I had created. In the same letter I wrote a plea for my father to accept some of the lifestyle choices of my siblings — an issue with which he has struggled for many years. As I closed the letter, a final verse to the song came to me...

I had an idea:

> *What if love was just like air*
>
> *and you could breathe it anywhere*
>
> *and never doubt that it was there;*
>
> *can't you just imagine?*

REFLECTION

1) What role does imagination play in your organization? In your life?

2) How are ideas, techniques, and technology used in your organization? In your life? How can you apply the "what if" question in both arenas?

3) Has imagination ever gotten you into trouble? Has it ever gotten you out of trouble?

Winning Isn't Everything

"Put me in, coach;
I'm ready to play!"

JOHN FOGERTY

Part 1 (The Rules of the Game)

IF your institution is like most, you're probably acclimated to following the rules. Decisions on personnel, purchasing, financial management, construction, computer security, and many other aspects of your daily life are based on policy and procedure.

That is, of course, unless you're involved with intercollegiate athletics.

Oh sure, they have policies and procedures as well. It's just that they seem to be able to do some things that the rest of us can't. Imagine if you will how life would be different if student affairs resembled intercollegiate athletics...

"In a surprising press release earlier today, Gipper College announced that all student affairs units would be merged with intercollegiate athletics. Film at eleven ..."

We'd be considered coaches instead of departmental directors. The department's head coach would have overall responsibility for the departmental team, supported by assistant coaches overseeing the offensive and defensive lines and perhaps a special teams unit. The offensive team (no pun intended) would be responsible for making progress and working toward goals. The defensive team would guard against threats and incursions from other teams (so much for collaboration ...). Special teams would be in charge of kicking off projects, running back initiatives, and trying to make extra points with the opposition, whoever they may be. And just to be safe, we'd always keep certain team members in reserve or on the bench. Team members would be selected only for specialized skills on one of these teams:

"She was our first-round draft choice for substance abuse counseling. We had to trade two hall directors to get her, but she's worth it ... ."

At many schools, the departmental coach would be seen driving a late-model auto from one of the local car dealerships. Boosters would abound, showering the department with scholarships, grants, and other less visible forms of support. Professional organizations would watch from the sidelines, making sure that none of the team members received inappropriate gifts from the boosters:

"Honest, coach. I didn't know that getting an interest-free loan from my bank compromised my role as a financial aid counselor."

Effective coaches would supplement their salaries with endorsements. Since shoes are already covered, we could branch out in some new directions. Toilet paper, perhaps. Maybe condoms. Personal hygiene could be big:

"Hello. I'm Joe Maternal, head coach of the university center at Gipper College, and I want to tell you what my team uses to prevent hemorrhoids."

When a coaching position would become vacant, we wouldn't have to bother with a search. A few phone calls, an innuendo or two in the newspaper, and the position would be filled — within a matter of days, not months:

"In a surprise announcement earlier today, Gipper College indicated that it had selected a new defensive coordinator for multicultural student services. Film at eleven ... ."

The departmental head coach would receive special training in the use of clichés. Prior to budget hearings, he would describe his team as having its back against the wall. At orientation, the team would go out there and play like there's no tomorrow. Up against student protest, it would be a do-or-die situation. Imagine the two-minute drill to complete goals and objectives:

"The auditors gave us a full court press, but we went into a zone defense and held them off ... ."

Dealing with the press would be an ongoing responsibility of the departmental head coach. Some might even have non-prime-time programs to review the past week's performance:

"Well, Biff, we've got a young team, and this year we're going to concentrate on the fundamentals. First and foremost, we're building character. We've got spirit, but we need experience if we're going to be competitive in this conference."

If the head coach had a particularly good year, he or she would have no problem getting a contract extension. On the other hand, a losing season could result in the fans (students) sending a moving van to the house. If the team didn't perform as desired, the head coach and all of the coaching staff could be fired without notice:

"In an announcement earlier today that surprised no one, Gipper College confirmed that it had fired head coach Wanda Waitlist. For a live report, we take you now to our on-the-scene reporter, Ima Luzer."

"Thank you, Biff. After a season marked by low turnout and controversy over illegal student recruiting practices, Gipper College gave admission coach Wanda "Lefty" Waitlist her walking papers. Speculation is high that her replacement may very well be Regina N. Rollem, known to most of our viewers as the Sultan of SAT. Both coaches were unavailable for comment. Back to you, Biff … ."

Our language is filled with sports imagery, and many sports expressions can be applied to our daily work in student affairs and higher education. We speak of "ballpark figures." When things go well, we hit a "home run." When they don't, we "strike out." If we're not careful, we can be "blitzed." If we don't pay attention, we're "out in left field." Every now and then we have to "call time out." The "clock's always running." We try to keep "personal fouls" to a minimum so that we can stay in the game.

Conversely, there aren't many T-shirts, posters, or coffee mugs emblazoned with student affairs language. It's hard to picture Nike changing its motto to "Just learn it," or characters in movies saying, "Show me the integrity." Wheaties probably won't become the "breakfast of scholars." Bubble gum cards of student affairs figures, complete with stats, are unlikely:

"I'll trade you my rookie card of Sandy "Koufax" Astin for your Art "Monk" Chickering pro bowl shot."

"Throw in your vintage Carole 'Island' Gilligan and it's a deal."

"Student development is life: the rest is just details." Now there's a sweatshirt slogan for you.

"Mom, Dad! I finally lettered in student involvement. I can't wait to get my jacket!"

"We're proud of you, son!"

Chances are, we'll never have our own cable network. On the other hand, we may not need press agents, image consultants, or personal representatives either:

"OK, Leroy, here's the deal. Alaska State is offering you seven million for three years."

"What's the catch?"

"It's a live-in position."

"No way, man. I won't do live-in for less than ten."

———•◦•———

If student affairs resembled intercollegiate athletics, winning wouldn't be everything: it would be the only thing (or so proclaimed the famous coach). Aphorisms would abound.

Fortunately, the student affairs milieu differs from athletics. The won-lost column doesn't determine our ethos and our objectives.

Or does it?

In the preceding satire, it was not my intention to malign any of our intercollegiate athletics colleagues. In a previous essay ("The Definite Article"), I made it a point to avoid stereotyping groups. Mea culpa. We do share certain qualities and aspirations with athletics. We continually strive for excellence in our programs. Constant improvement is a common denominator. We attempt to develop the leadership potential of all of our players. Much of our time is spent in the public arena. We try to make sure the playing field is level. We work toward common goals, trying to avoid the penalties and turnovers that come with breaking the rules or not effectively playing our positions. We frequently have to huddle up to strategize our next move. Sometimes it's enough to go for the short yardage; sometimes we have to go deep. If we don't stretch and condition ourselves, we won't be in shape when the pressure's on.

Winning isn't everything; win-win is better. We're not coaches, but we need to practice coaching. We work best when we work as a team.

Part 2 (Put Me in, Coach)

I was never much of an athlete. This statement comes as no surprise to anyone who's ever met me. When they handed out the athletic genes, I was in another room listening to music.

The very first time I carried a football in an eighth-grade intramural game, I saw a huge hole in the line and ran for it. Somewhere in the pile of bodies on the ground, a hand reached out and grabbed my left foot. I think it was the hand of fate. My body turned 180 degrees but my left foot didn't. I was carried off the field in agony and never went back. When they handed out athletic ability, I was watching a Saturday matinee.

I played intramural basketball in high school, accumulating a grand total of four points (not baskets: four points) for the season. In college, I successfully avoided most contact with sports, though I did attend one football game. One semester on the staff bowling league in graduate school reconfirmed my lack of gross motor skills. When they handed out athletic enthusiasm, I was reading a good book.

Golf? Too dangerous. I've only played twice but it was enough to have me banned from all golf courses for life. Carts are kind of fun. I'd much prefer just driving the cart on a fine trimmed lawn and forget about trying to use a bent piece of metal to hit a ball into the lake or the woods. When they handed out athletic talent, I was writing a song.

Last summer, I decided I'd give sports one last chance — slowpitch softball. In a church league. With several men much older than me. What could be easier and more enjoyable? Perhaps oral surgery.

The first time out wasn't too bad. I actually got a hit my first time at bat. I made it to first without needing oxygen. A long drive by the next batter got me to third. When I crossed home plate after the next batter grounded out, I thought I'd truly reached home! Piece of cake.

Put me in, coach.

Since I was the new guy and the team manager didn't know my skills, I was sent to right field. Not a bad place to be, since most of the right-handers hit into left field. When the first left-hander came up, everyone motioned for me to move back. I took a few steps backward, then waited, glove on knee as I'd learned years before. I heard the crack of the bat, saw the ball ascending, and all too late realized it was far above my head. Uttering a word not frequently heard in church league softball, I chased after the first of several balls from left-handed hitters. They'd found their spot.

I was moved to first base in the next game. I still felt sore from the game a few nights earlier, but my new glove did the job. Up to bat, I waited for just the right pitch, hit it well, and knew it would land beyond the infielders and short of the outfielders. Wearing my new baseball cleats, I dropped the bat and started sprinting for first.

I made it about five yards.

It felt as if someone with large tongs had reached in below the skin on my thighs, grabbed the muscles there, and pulled them off of the thighbones.

Quads, they call them. A muscle group I didn't know I had that I apparently hadn't adequately conditioned or stretched. Pulled quads occur frequently with men my age. If you don't use 'em, you pull 'em. It might happen to women as well, but I think women are clearly more intelligent than men are. You don't hear about them pulling their quads very often.

I sat out the rest of the game icing my quads.

Not one to give up so easily, I made an appointment with our campus fitness coordinator, who prescribed a regimen of exercise and stretching. I worked for three weeks to prepare, got to the game early, went through a series of stretching exercises, and psyched myself for my big comeback.

Put me in, coach.

He suggested moving me to catcher. Why not? I was there for the team. I soon discovered that the ball, so large and bright to the batter, was actually rather hard to catch in slowpitch. It drops like a rock and always bounces in a direction opposite from what you anticipate. After a couple of innings, though, I was starting to get the hang of it.

No outs. Runner on second base. Batter with one strike, two balls. The pitch comes in, high and slow. I know the batter's going for it. The ball's a little too high, but the batter swings and connects. It's a line drive, slightly to the right of the pitcher. Instead of reaching for it with the glove on his left hand, he reaches out his bare right hand. The ball smacks his hand and keeps on going. The runner is well on his way to first. The pitcher is shaking his hand feverishly. The runner on second base has reached third, and it looks like he's going to keep coming. The second baseman realizes it's too late to throw the runner out at first. He picks up the ball and fires it home. The runner keeps on coming but it's clear the ball is going to get there first. It does.

About three inches below my glove.

On my left shin.

The ball bounces away, the runner scores, and I hop after it to keep the batter from going past second.

Next inning, I'm at bat. Good clean hit to left field. The first base coach tells me to keep going. I round first base and the earth seems to disappear beneath my feet. In what feels like slow motion, I fly and fall for an eternity. I hit the ground. Hard. In a huge cloud of dust, I scramble back to my feet and somehow make it to second base. There's a spot on my right shoulder where the blood is visible through the shirt, but it's my left shin that grabs my attention. A huge goose egg — more like a pterodactyl egg — has formed where the ball hit me previously. I couldn't believe something so large and disgusting could suddenly just appear on my body. The coach sends in a designated runner. Again. I find my way back to the bench and the ice. Again. Take me out, coach.

The greatest shame came not from my teammates or my opponents. They were sympathetic, helpful, and quick with suggestions for reducing the swelling. A player from the other team suffered a broken collarbone and our pitcher's hand swelled to the size of a catcher's glove in the same game, so there was an espirit de corps among the middle-aged men physically injuring themselves in a child's game. After all, winning isn't everything. No, the greatest shame came when I presented myself to my wife after I got home. Bruised, battered, and bloodied. Covered with sweat, dirt, and grass stains. The look in her eyes said it all.

"But we won," I explained, like a little boy trying to justify ruining his new shoes in a sandlot scrimmage.

She just shook her head.

As I understand it, I won't be allowed to play again next summer unless I lose a little weight and spend the entire year training and conditioning. She's a tough general manager.

Seen any good movies lately?

Part 3 (The Final Score)

Winning isn't everything. In the grand scheme of things, in life's rich pageant, winning isn't important at all. Don't let the athletic shoe commercials tell you that winning is everything; they just want you to buy their shoes. Winning isn't everything. It isn't love or happiness or satisfaction or contentment or personal achievement or friendship or beauty or truth. Playing is more important than winning. Losing graciously is more important than winning. A soft September night with just a trace of autumn in the breeze, surrounded by friends and food, watching a high school or college game is a winning combination — even if the home team doesn't make the most points. Winning isn't everything, and it sure as hell isn't the only thing.

The won-lost column doesn't determine our ethos and our objectives.

Or does it?

Put me in, coach. We can't lose.

REFLECTION

1) Which qualities of an athletic program should student affairs departments emulate? Which qualities should not be emulated?

2) Should we, in our work, attempt to counter societal messages about winning? If so, how can we do that?

3) What are some examples of won-lost records in student affairs?

Floor Finishes

"One man's ceiling is
Another man's floor."

PAUL SIMON

*Caution: a significant number of painful puns
follow. Reader discretion is advised.*

HAVE you ever noticed the many references
in our language to *floors*? More than a
metafloor, floors provide the *foundation* for so
much of what we do. Allow me to *wax* philosophical for just a moment.

Floor.

It's a funny little word, sitting there all by itself.
It even takes on different sounds: it can rhyme
with newer, core, or mar, depending on your
accent and dialect. Say it several times in a row
and you'll begin to wonder if it's really a word
at all.

We seem to have a fascination for floor-based
expressions. What is the *basis* (*i.e.*, *bedrock*,
ground, *root*, or *footing*) for our floor fixation?
Of greater importance, can we look at floors in
a new way as a metaphor for our work? Let me
start at the *bottom* and work my way up.

———※———

Floor plans. Most of us in student affairs are
familiar with floor plans, through our work
with renovation projects and office moves.
Floor plans are a simple, two-dimensional way

to envision physical space. Technology is expanding our capacity: virtual reality is beginning to allow people to virtually walk through a room before it's actually constructed. Some of us wonder if we'll continue to create spaces as interesting as those developed before the age of virtual virtuosity. In the meantime, we have our *physical* floor plans.

Students and staff also need *metaphysical* floor plans. They need to conceptualize the institution as an integrated place where one room logically leads to the next. They need to know that there is a plan, that the institution can be navigated without running into blind corners and walls. They also need to see the floor plans so that they can conceptualize where new rooms ought to be, where new passageways can be created, and where their ideas can contribute to the architecture of the greater organization.

Giving someone the floor. If you've ever been on a committee or attended a meeting, giving someone the floor is a familiar concept. Actually, when we give someone the floor, she or he actually winds up taking the whole room — or at least the majority of the air in it. What if we had to literally give someone the floor? More than our participles would be dangling. Rather than *giving* someone the floor, perhaps we should *share* it; that way, we'd *literally* have a common *under-standing*.

Students and staff need to be given the floor *figuratively*. They need to have a forum in which their voices can be heard, sometimes in solo performance and sometimes in harmony with other voices. They need to be heard and we need to listen, even if their needs must be addressed elsewhere. They need to have meaningful roles in the life and decision-making processes of the institution. They need to learn to use the floor, share the floor, and give the floor to others.

Floorshows. With all due respect, floors aren't very interesting. We walk all over them. If I go to a show, I want to see what's happening a little higher up than the floor. Casinos have floorshows; I suppose they're there to distract you while all your money goes down the *drain*. If carpet companies had floorshows, they could make a *pile* of money (that's an old yarn ...). Speaking of carpet, what does it really mean to be *called on the carpet*? I assume it has something to do with the fact that you end up looking at the floor while someone — a parent or a supervisor — is yelling at you. Every day, *extemporaneous* floorshows go on all around us.

Students and staff are the *veritable* floorshow in higher education. Their opportunity to perform is our reason for being. The stars in the classroom and across the campus should be the students, not their instructors or advisors. We should never cease to be amazed, amused, entertained, and enlightened by their performances. The show must go on.

Coming in on the ground floor. This common business expression states the obvious.

Start at the beginning. Work up from the bottom. First things first. It's hard to imagine coming in anywhere *but* the ground floor, though some may try. I suppose you can come in on the basement floor if you've got the right equipment and *tunnel vision*. Through inheritance, some folks start out on a higher floor. For most of us, it's more *pragmatic* to come in on the ground floor.

Students and staff *essentially* come in on the ground floor. Everyone coming to the institution is starting over, whether freshman, transfer student, new faculty member, classified employee, or administrator. Everyone wonders if they'll fit. Everyone wants to belong. Everyone makes mistakes in adjusting to the new culture. Not everyone survives. Some seek the cool comfort and anonymity of the basement; some seek the power and visibility of the ivory towers. Many find themselves on the middle floors, doing what needs to be done. But everyone essentially comes in on the ground floor.

A SHORT QUIZ:

1) Is there something beneath the floor or is it joist my imagination?

2) If your carpet is back ordered, are you out of the loop?

3) Do fitness centers buff their floors?

4) Do delis have sub-floors?

OK, so maybe my platform is missing a few planks. Some of this, after all, was meant to be *tongue in grooved cheek*. If these puns have you floored, or if you're climbing the walls and going through the roof (as opposed to rolling in the aisles), there is a point in all of this.

Actually, floors are fairly important to our world of work. The physical appearance of our floors is an important factor in people's perceptions. A worn, stained, or outdated floor compromises a wonderfully furnished room. Sooner or later people look down, and they're apt to make judgments about you, your staff, and your programs based on what they see.

What type of floor do you need? A well-maintained, wooden floor provides any room with a sense of quality, durability, and timeliness. Carpeting can soften a room, improve its acoustics, and add color and warmth to the furnishings. Terrazzo, while expensive and difficult to install, creates a sense of permanence and resilience in appropriate settings.

Floors should have character. Floors should hold up under excessive traffic. Floors should complement but not outshine the other functions of the room.

Given proper maintenance, floors should last a long time. Floors should be timeless, not trendy. Floors provide support.

What kind of floor are you?

REFLECTION

1) If you were a floor, what type would you be (e.g., wood parquet, wall-to-wall carpet, ceramic tile, wooden planks, carpet tiles, poured terrazzo, sheet vinyl, etc.)? Why?

2) If you had the opportunity and resources, would you change any of the floors in your facilities (literally or figuratively)? Why?

3) In the next to the last paragraph of this essay, several qualities of good flooring are listed. How would each of the qualities (e.g., character, endurance, integration, maintenance, stability, and support) apply to your role in your organization?

Ringo, the Packers, 007, and Me

"What do you do when your

dreams come true

And they're not quite like you planned?"

DON HENLEY AND GLENN FREY

AS a child, I'm quite sure I never told anyone that I wanted to be a university center director when I grew up. In the decade of the Beatles, James Bond, and Bart Starr, the preferable career choices for a boy like me were rock star, secret agent, and quarterback.

I didn't have the hair, the talent, or the connections to become an arena rocker, but I did play in a bar band for several years. I wasn't suave and debonair like the man from U.N.C.L.E., although I'm pretty good at keeping secrets. I was cut from the football team, but I did play first-chair tuba in the pep band.

My destiny awaited elsewhere.

I never met a university center director — never even knew that such a person existed — until my first year in college. It seemed like a pretty decent job: nice offices with plenty of cool audio-visual equipment continually surrounded by people like me (students).

Three years of working in a university center setting took its toll on me, and I decided to become a director when I grew up.

My career path was nothing extraordinary: two years of preparation in graduate school, three years as a student activities program advisor, two years as a university center assistant director in charge of facilities, four years as an associate director, then a move to a new school to become director of activities and the campus center. It took me eleven years to reach my goal, but I was who and where I wanted to be.

I was fortunate, worked hard, and eventually achieved my goal of becoming a university center director, and I enjoyed the opportunities that came my way through involvement in professional organizations. In my career plans, such as they were, I never really imagined being anything but a university center director.

For eight years, I was who and where I wanted to be.

Near the end of that time period, my department — known then as the Office of Student Activities — underwent a process of review, reflection, and speculation that resulted in significant changes in organizational nature and scope. We realized that higher education was beginning a period of revolutionary change, that our university was poised to be a leader in those changes, and that we could determine our importance and value to the campus rather than waiting to be told what to do next. We changed our name to reflect the central role of our programs and services to the entire university: we became the University Center. We developed the concept of a leadership center based on outcomes and learning rather than activities. We re-emphasized the importance of quality service, "one-stop shopping" for our customers, and new ways of looking at our facilities as flexible, dynamic places where new ideas could be brought to life. We incorporated conference services into a new event planning concept and sought new ways to deliver services to students, staff, and guests of the university. We brought Greek life into the family, gave commuting students an expanded home, and provided an important organizational connection for Student Government. We developed new ideas for the maintenance and housekeeping of our facilities, expanded the capabilities of our theater, and developed much better methods for managing our budgets. We made student learning and quality service the primary building blocks on which all of our efforts were constructed. We inherited the orientation program and changed its focus from primarily social assimilation to primarily educational matriculation. We helped the Division of Student Affairs embrace change by modeling effective change management in our department.

These accomplishments didn't go unpunished.

I was asked to step away from this role for an indefinite period of time to work on other university priorities. I was given an opportunity — something a friend of mine called "an internship for life" — to learn about another area of the university, to develop new connections within and beyond the division. I was served a plate full of opportunities to nurture, challenges to overcome, questions to ask and answer, concerns to address, and potential mistakes to make. I would, hopefully, continue to contribute to an ever-changing environment, in a new role.

On the one hand, I was flattered to be given the opportunity to advance, to learn new skills and develop new competencies, and to move up the organizational ladder, and I was looking forward to working with colleagues in new, developing relationships. On the other hand, it meant stepping away from the people and the department that had meant so much to me, leaving behind the comfortable and familiar and engaging the challenges and possibilities.

It meant not being the university center director anymore.

The goal for which I'd prepared for eleven years. The goal that I'd lived for eight years. This was no dream deferred; it was a dream realized.

And it was over.

What happens after you've reached your goals, after you've realized your dream? I hadn't spent a great deal of time thinking about that.

One answer is to set new goals and dream new dreams.

Too easy.

There's an empty place, somewhere between the end of one dream and the beginning of another, and I found myself there, unexpectedly, through no definitive plan of my own. I found myself advancing along a career path that passed my destination. I looked back occasionally but could no longer see where I'd been.

In this empty place, you miss the old dream. You miss the dreaming that resulted in the realized dream. You miss the satisfaction you found when the dream came true. You cognitively understand that new dreams are possible, but you affectively believe that there will never be a dream to replace the realized dream.

Eventually, though, you wake up and start working on new goals, new dreams.

At a national conference, I ran into a colleague going through a similar experience. He too was grieving the end of a realized goal. Unfortunately, he was only looking back; I was beginning to look ahead. I'd set some new goals, and the new dreams were beginning to crystallize. I hope he found his way out of that empty place.

We rarely think about what lies beyond our goals. We're so focused on hitting our targets that we're surprised when our arrows pass through them and into the woods beyond.

There's an "even later" that follows the "happily ever after."

I'm no expert in karate, but I understand the essential value of seeing beyond the stack of wood through which your hand must pass. A fairly good golf enthusiast I know tells me that shooting slightly beyond the hole is the best bet; short putts never fall in the hole. I can't break through a stack of wood or sink a long putt, but the metaphor isn't lost on me.

The Beatles live on in music and the occasional re-release of archive material. James Bond is in yet another incarnation of British actor. Quarterbacks have short-lived athletic careers, then open restaurants and car dealerships. University center directors, I've learned, have many options. Like staying put. Or getting kicked upstairs. Or moving into the private sector. Or moving to larger schools with larger facilities. Or writing books.

Jimmy Buffett, the belated pirate, sings: "Where it all ends, I can't fathom my friends, if I did I'd have to throw out my anchor." If I had an anchor I'd be tempted to join him. In the meantime, I'll sail these seas beyond the horizons I set for myself. Maybe the career that follows the one I chose to be when I grew up is out there waiting for me. To quote my over-quoted favorite musician, Jackson Browne: "We'll see how far this new road reaches."

My destiny awaits somewhere.

REFLECTION

1) What are some of the dreams or goals that you've gone beyond? What can you do about it now?

2) What "life internships" have you experienced? How have you dealt with them?

3) Is your career path a one-way, dead end street? If so, what can you do to change that? And if not, how might you keep it from becoming one?

Directors

"It's my job to be worried half to death
But that's the thing people respect in me.
It's my job, but without it, I'd be less
Than what I expect from me."

MAC McANALLY

"WHAT is a director?"

To some extent, it depends on whom you ask. I've been one. I know many. Some report to me. Many aspire to the role. It's an important job on any campus. Still, there's something elusive about the title and the role. How does *my* understanding of the term correlate to *others'* understanding?

In this essay, I'm going to do two things. First, I'm going to reinforce the notion of perspective as it relates to the position. Then I'm going to offer working definitions of two significant aspects of the job: the functional and the organizational. Why? Because I've been a director, I know many of them, some report to me, and many aspire to the role. It's an important job and somebody has to do it.

Part 1: Perspectives on Position

Perspective is a fascinating thing. Imagine a group of people, sitting around a campfire on a cool autumn evening. Although each person is looking at the same fire, they're all experiencing it in different ways. Because of the location of each seat, the shape of the fire will be different; perhaps the heat and the direction of the smoke will be different as well. Additionally, each person sees the fire through his or her own experience; the fire evokes memories of previous campfires, fear of burns, smells of childhood, recollections of relationships — any number of possible thoughts and reminiscences. Perspective, then, is not the fire; it's how each person perceives the fire.

When we examine directors or any other level of management, we have to be cognizant of perspectives. If our understanding of the position is going to be something more than superficial or one-dimensional, we need to put the position in the perspective of all who have expectations of the position.

Case in point: A colleague (and a director) asked the graduate students in his college student personnel administration class to answer the question, "What is a director?" Their responses — their perspectives — provide valuable and interesting insights on the director position. I've compiled several of their comments and created themes to capture the essence of these perceptions: martyr, mentor, magician, mediator, and mirror (alliteration is alive!).

The martyr. "Part of being a director, I think, is adopting a willingness to have days when you feel a little worn down." "The student affairs director may be called on to be all things to all people and receive very little institutional recognition for active leadership." "I see the director as the person who will pick up the slack when times get tough and overwhelming." "In some ways, directors are regarded by so many as the role model or mentor that they give up the right to have a bad day." "They are setting the tone of the office, so ideally the director hums even on those days when it's difficult to love what they do."

In other words, some of our days are real hummers!

The mentor. "I think of the department as a team and the director as the one who encourages, supports, and provides the game plan for how the team will win." "I believe that directors are the teachers of not only their staff but of all the individuals with whom they come into daily contact." "A director anticipates and sometimes initiates change — whatever it takes to reach students and help them grow developmentally and intellectually." "A director must be a communicator, a mission caster, an equipper of people, an accountant, and, most importantly, a team player." "I think a director is more of a leader than an expert."

How many of us confuse those last two characteristics?

The magician. "A director wears many hats and must wear them all very well." "They are expected to know all of the answers and never have to ask any of the questions." "Directors must be flexible but they also must be able to make smart decisions quickly." "To me, a director is a supervisor who makes sure that everything runs smoothly." "The great challenge of a director is to master the marvelous balancing act between advocating and disciplining, between head and heart, and between challenge and support."

Done any juggling lately?

The mediator. "A director is, in some ways, a *go between* who has the responsibility of interacting with a wide spectrum of individuals on campus." "Much of the responsibility of a director focuses on acting as an advocate for office staff." "It is the intangible qualities, such as personality, approachability, availability, and others, which change an effective director to an outstanding director." "Plainly, the director should insure that everyone is on the same page."

Sometimes it's enough to get everyone reading in the same book!

The mirror. "Ultimately, the qualities of the director will reflect the values and beliefs of the organization." "The director communicates the vision of the office, inside and outside of the university." "The challenge for directors is to have enough of a Gestalt understanding of the big picture of the campus and higher education in general so that they understand the far-reaching implications of decisions they make." "Directors should be seen and sometimes *not* heard."

Don't you just love the last quote?

The graduate assistants who provided these comments are just one potential point of perspective. It would be interesting and worthwhile to discover how others on campus — particularly students — perceive the role. What perceptions does the president have? The faculty? The subordinates of the director? (See "The Role of Roles" elsewhere in this book.) Finally, what perspectives do directors themselves have regarding their jobs? Maybe we should ask.

Part Two: Functional and Organizational Definitions

"What is a director?"

Having spent the better part of the last ten years with that title, I found it interesting when that question came up during a conversation with the chief student affairs officer on my campus. At the time, I was in an acting position supervising five other directors, people who just previously had been my peers, my organizational equals.

The term "director" came into question as our organization grew. In some instances, there were directors reporting to directors who were reporting to assistant or associate vice presidents — who in turn reported to a vice president. Periodically, a director would be in a direct reporting line with the vice president. Some directors had responsibility for large staffs, extensive physical plant, and complex budgets; others worked with smaller staffs, offices, and budgets. Some operated auxiliary services; others managed educational services. The common ground between people carrying the director title seemed obscure at best.

I was surprised to learn that a commonly accepted belief about directors at my institution could be summarized in the expression, "A director is anyone who reports to an associate vice president." The statement reflected a hierarchical perspective, *i.e.*, the title was determined by status and not necessarily by accountability; by whom you reported to, not by what you did.

I disagreed.

I thought there had to be a better description of the roles I'd played as a director, the relationships I'd formed on campus, and the responsibility and accountability I'd assumed. I believed that we could, in fairly descriptive language, communicate *what a director does* and *what is expected of a director.* Furthermore, I didn't think any position could be defined solely in terms of its relationship to the supervisor of that position!

To answer the question in a more satisfactory way, I turned to written position descriptions, performance appraisal, and personal experience. And I concluded that the title could be defined both *functionally* and *organizationally.*

A **functional** definition of the role addresses what is expected of the position from above, below, and across the campus in terms of competency, level of performance, etc. An **organizational** definition addresses how organizational priorities, political considerations, restructuring, and institutional dynamics affect the role in terms of reporting relationship, scope of responsibility, etc. To make sense out of the position, both definitions are critical.

The functional definition of director. In formulating a functional definition, I considered common expectations that should reasonably be held for someone at the director level. Accountability is the key consideration: the director is ultimately accountable for planning, leadership, staffing, measurement, communication, and coordination at the departmental level. While others share in the responsibility for these functions, the director is ultimately accountable to the institution and its constituents — as well as to the individuals within the unit — for accomplishing these functions. The point to be made here is that these functions should be associated with the director regardless of the organizational context: *these are the things that directors do.*

Many of these functions listed below can be found in performance appraisals and job descriptions. Others came from discussions with colleagues, personal experience, and some very old lecture notes from graduate school. I'm sure I've left out some important considerations, and there may be some here with which you disagree. I offer these as a jumping-off point for further discussion.

*Directors are accountable for **planning** at the departmental level.* The director:

- directs the development of short-, intermediate-, and long-range planning related to university and divisional missions.
- sets objectives and priorities based on university and division goals.
- leads the department in developing individual and unit goals in support of division and university goals.

- develops strategies and work plans for accomplishing goals.

- coordinates and assumes accountability for the acquisition and use of university resources at the departmental level (financial, human, facilities, equipment, materials).

- anticipates, identifies, and responds to problems and issues related to departmental functions.

- organizes tasks in logical sequences and identifies required resources.

- investigates new methodologies and technologies that may impact on the effectiveness of departmental functions.

*Directors are accountable for **leadership** at the departmental level.* The director:

- promotes productive, creative working environments.

- maintains high performance standards under pressure.

- develops and implements new and improved ways of accomplishing objectives.

- understands procedures, policies, and responsibilities of functional areas.

- interacts with others to achieve university goals.

- acquires and maintains a body of knowledge and expertise in higher education and student affairs, as well as functional expertise.

- balances autonomy with interdependence (can manage independently if necessary but chooses to collaborate whenever possible).

*Directors are accountable for **staffing** at the departmental level.* The director:

- recruits, selects, develops, and assimilates a diverse staff.

- staffs the functional area with the appropriate number and mix of employees.

- creatively addresses staff shortages, vacancies, etc.

- delegates authority and responsibility to efficiently and effectively achieve goals.

- supports staff in increasing their capabilities to contribute and develop.

- identifies departmental training and professional development needs.

*Directors are accountable for **measurement** at the departmental level.* The director:

- initiates and facilitates departmental measurement, including needs assessment, outcomes assessment, program evaluation, and performance appraisal.

- provides staff with ongoing feedback and coaching.

- facilitates recognition efforts within the functional area.

Directors are accountable for **communication** *at the departmental, divisional, and university levels.* The director:

- communicates departmental priorities and issues to the broader university community.

- prepares and maintains reports, statistics, and presentations related to the functional area.

- facilitates the flow of information inside and beyond the functional area.

Directors are accountable for **coordination** *at the departmental, divisional, and university levels.* The director:

- serves on divisional and university committees, missions, and task forces.

- provides coordination with other offices to insure the availability of services and to avoid duplication of services.

- provides information and professional judgment to other division and university personnel related to student needs, interests, and issues.

- participates in the functions of the division and supports staff participation in divisional functions.

The organizational definition of director. Beyond the functions expected of a director, organizational settings pose unique challenges and opportunities for the individual filling the position. The organizational definition focuses on the relationship of the director to the organization. Although common expectations exist for all directors, each director is in a different position representing a different discipline with different responsibilities; directors are unique in relation to the organization. The institution and its divisions dictate where directors are located in the organizational structure, but to whom they report is circumstantial at best.

Additionally, each institution has its own set of conditions, organizational issues, history, and culture that bear on the organizational status and role of the director. Mandates, politics, interdivisional conflict, restructuring initiatives, the president's interest and support (or lack thereof) — these considerations have an impact on the organizational nature of the director's position.

Do effectiveness and productivity or uniformity and serenity motivate the organization? Is accountability a higher value than status? What role does tradition play in the organizational consideration of the position? If the director title has proliferated without consideration to the functions listed above, what other language can be employed to represent levels of leadership and management within the organization (*i.e.,* what distinguishes a director from a coordinator)? Does the director title reflect a level of management or a level of leadership?

One of the graduate students in my colleague's class made an interesting observation that captures the organizational definition of the director:

"Today in the area of student affairs, directors are faced with the challenge of creating their own definition based on the needs of the organization."

In other words, effective directors must be capable of *functioning* in an *organizational* context, regardless of *perspective*. How do I know this? Because I've been a director, I know many of them, some report to me, and many aspire to the role. It's an important job — and I'm glad I got to do it.

REFLECTION

1) Martyr, mentor, magician, mediator, and mirror: how accurately do these metaphors reflect the role of directors on your campus?

2) Does the director title reflect a level of management or a level of leadership at your institution? Do various constituencies (e.g., students, faculty, parents, boards, etc.) have differing perspectives on which role is played by directors?

3) What is your perspective on associate or assistant director positions?

Double Rubs

"Then your wife seems to think
That you're part of the furniture
Oh, it's peculiar ..."

SUPERTRAMP

SO I married an interior decorator.

I didn't know it at the time. Neither did she.

I was an English major with a Business minor. She majored in Home Economics with a focus on textiles.

We met in a bar. That was over twenty years ago and we're still going strong. It can happen.

I played bass in the jazz trio at the Holiday Inn. She worked as a waitress. In this way we partially financed our undergraduate educations. During the summer of 1975, we met, went on a picnic, and fell in love — and the rest is history. And herstory.

I started a graduate program in college student personnel administration and she went to work selling kitchen cabinets. I wrote my paper and studied for comps while she fell in with a band of interior designers. I began my first job in student activities as she sold floor coverings. Our family started about the same time. I slowly climbed the organizational ladder while she studied solar energy and construction. When an incredible opportunity came my way to direct a growing department, she continued her experiential learning in interior design, working with an established company in our new town. Eventually, she made the leap into creating her own business.

Self-motivated, self-assured, and self-employed.

During her developmental process, I too benefited from her skills, knowledge, and competencies. Like many other student center directors, I didn't have a clue what I was looking for in terms of color selection, fabrics, wall coverings, floor coverings, and furnishings. To be honest, I made a few mistakes — some of them costly — until I started listening to and asking questions of my wife and others. What impact does color have on a room? Why use a semi-gloss paint instead of a flat finish? How can you tell if upholstery is going to stand up to the traffic experienced in a student center lounge? What do you do to make a cinder block wall look less institutional? Are carpet tiles a viable alternative? How can furniture produced in state correctional facilities — a mandatory consideration for many of us — be integrated with other furnishings to create a professional office setting?

I have to say that I've learned a great deal. I used to think *lambrekin* was the name of one of Sherri Lewis' puppets (somebody pulled the wool over my eyes ...). A *double rub* was probably a massage conducted by two Swedish masseuses (and it would be catastrophic if they rubbed you the wrong way ...). *Valance* was obviously the guy Jimmy Stewart had to shoot in that old western movie (I took a little liberty with that one ...). I'm a wiser man today. I now know that lambrekins and valances are types of window treatments, and that double rub, in layman's terms, indicates the potential durability of fabric.

If behavior is a function of the person's interaction with the environment, as Kurt Lewin and James Banning posited in *Student Services: A Handbook for the Profession*, it's probably wise that we make sure our environments are saying what we want them to say, doing what we want them to do, and working as we want them to work. We need to be as cognizant of environmental theory as we claim to be of developmental theory.

———

Double rub. It's an interesting concept. I sit on a sofa; I stand up. That's a double rub. I do it ten times; that's ten double rubs. A fabric with 5,000 double rubs will handle someone's rump about 5,000 times. If I estimate that a chair in my lounge will "seat" someone 20 times in a day, I can start thinking about reupholstering that chair after only 250 days of use. Chances are, I'll want to consider a fabric with substantially more than 5,000 double rubs for the lounge. A fabric with 50,000 double rubs may give me 2,500 days of use — over six years, barring floods, plagues, or pestilence.

I once made the mistake of furnishing an entire lounge in a beautiful fabric — with 5,000 double rubs. It looked great. A year later, we reupholstered several of the pieces.

When was the last time you checked the double rub potential of your furniture?

How about people; do we too have built in double rub numbers? How many times are we "sat on" in decision making or other work situations before we start to wear down or out? How many times can we be rubbed the wrong way by students, supervisors, guests, or co-workers before our stuffing and springs start to show? Can we be reupholstered through training and professional development? What kind of Scotch Guard™ works on humans to increase our resilience? (Too much Scotch and you lower your guard ...) Do we too fall out of fashion over time if we don't keep up with trends and issues in our field? Is there some way in the interview process to legally request an applicant's double rub potential?

Probably not. Still, it's something to think about.

———•◦•———

An effective environment requires the coordination of colors, textures, form, and function. An effective organization requires the coordination of colors, textures, form, and function. Coincidence? I don't think so.

Appearance is important, but skin-deep beauty is a price most of us can't afford. We've got to be practical.

Durability is necessary, but who wants to live in a sterile, impersonal environment? We've got to be inspired.

Balance — that's what we need. Aesthetics and durability, practicality and inspiration. Double rubs with style.

In our surroundings and in ourselves.

REFLECTION

1) What's your double rub potential with respect to work? How durable (emotionally, physically, spiritually) are you? What do you do when you begin to wear down?

2) Are your surroundings — personal and professional — based primarily on function, form, or both? Why? What are the consequences of favoring one over the other?

3) What role do aesthetics, durability, practicality, and inspiration play in your work? How do you find balance between form and function?

Leading the Gaggle

"When gray geese honk across
the autumn sky,
Will you look up and hear the call?"

DAVID BUSKIN

IN Fort Collins, Colorado, an eastern slope, Front Range community with an abundance of parks and greenbelts — and the home of Colorado State University — there's a beautiful lake in City Park close to the married student housing complex that I managed as a graduate assistant. This lake was within easy walking distance of the entire campus and was a winter home for a large gaggle of Canada Geese (not *Canadian* Geese, as I later learned, but *Canada* Geese). Like many of our residents and peers, my wife and I enjoyed watching them, feeding them, sharing in the joy of their newborn chicks, and observing their antics. We also learned how to step gingerly when crossing fields and lawns recently occupied by the large waterfowl.

We took for granted their presence, not realizing that this was in fact one of the major nesting spots for Canada Geese, a location where the geese had, over time, learned to coexist peacefully with humans, their dogs, and their children. Protected by city and state ordinances, the geese lived peacefully in our midst — or perhaps we lived peacefully in their midst.

Caught up in graduate school and the management of 350 apartments whose occupants represented numerous nationalities, I missed some important distinctions about these geese that researchers, naturalists, and novelists have captured and interpreted for our benefit. We migrated southward several years ago ourselves and never returned to that Front Range wild goose refuge. From time to time, I have come across geese in literature. Children's author Ron Hirschi (*City Geese*), the indefatigable James Michener (*Chesapeake*), fantasy writer T.H. White (*The Once and Future King*), and others have given us bird's eye views of the geese and their unique characteristics. Nonetheless, I never quite grasped the lessons of these birds as potentially applied to human relations and leadership.

Recently, while participating in a workshop on fundraising, I was reintroduced to my old feathered friends. The speaker, a minister with a strong regional reputation as a whiz in fundraising and leadership, had a difficult task. Most people — myself included — are about as enamored with fundraising as we are with crossing those fields after the geese have done their business. Making this unpleasant task more palatable was his objective, and he used a few "fowl facts" to teach us some consequential lessons on leadership.

Shared leadership. First, we learned that Canada Geese always fly in the "V" formation that we associate with waterfowl. Even children are aware of this phenomenon, although when we were kids we perhaps hadn't realized that it isn't the same goose at the head of the "V" all the time. Each goose takes its turn at the point. Michener's "Onk-Or" demonstrated that the "V" is aerodynamically the best possible way for the geese to fly — short of first-class seats on a jumbo jet. The further back in line the geese fly, the less wind resistance they face. Since the lead goose must work particularly hard to cut through the wind, the other geese must also take their turns at this position.

This is an example in the natural world of shared leadership, one of the most important aspects of contemporary leadership and citizenship models. Like the geese, none of us can be in front all of the time; to reach our destination, we need to rotate all of our gaggle through to this position.

"I just flew in from L.A., and boy are my arms tired."

Next time, try flying in the "V" formation and rotating the leadership. At the very least, you'll end up with fewer ruffled feathers.

Keeping company with the fallen. Most of us were unaware that Canada Geese are incredibly loyal; they mate for life. If a companion, through injury or exhaustion, is forced to the ground, other geese will accompany that fallen goose to the ground, staying with it until it can rejoin the larger group, offering protection, even giving their own lives in defense of the fallen goose. For survival purposes, these birds have learned to keep company with the fallen.

Many of us would consider this a "humane" act. When comrades fall, they need the support of the group to find their wings (or, in a human context, to get back on their feet). To return to the larger group, a small "V" formation is required.

Geese have this figured out; why is it so difficult for us humans to understand? When we see colleagues and co-workers struggling, do we double back to help or do we try to put some distance between our fallen comrades and ourselves? To whom are we loyal?

Stick around. Your reward for providing aid to your colleagues is the emotional equivalent of finding the goose that lays golden eggs. Your gaggle gets the benefit of having a stronger team with deeper emotional ties — and you get the benefit of knowing that the gaggle will be there for you, should you ever need its aid and comfort.

Honking encouragement. The last attribute, though I'm sure there are others that we have yet to discover, has to do with sound. If you've ever been around Canada Geese, you know they're capable of making a loud, obnoxious (to some) clatter as they fly. The geese all honk as they migrate.

All but one, that is.

The goose at the head of the "V" is using so much energy to cut through the wind that it can't use any of its strength to honk. The rest of the geese are communicating with the leader, letting the leader know that they're right behind, urging the leader onward. To reach their goal, the followers have learned to honk encouragement from behind, giving the leader the inspiration to keep on flying toward the destination until it's time for another leader to take the leadership position.

We've all been there — flapping our wings, trying with all our might to reach the goal. It's so much better when someone's behind you or beside you with words of encouragement and moral support — someone honking, "Way to go, keep it up, you're doing great!" How often do we honk encouragement to those leading our gaggle? Is it easier to mumble criticism, second guess the leader, and tell others how much better we could do it?

Maybe we all just need to be goosed every now and then ... but in a good way.

REFLECTION

1) How can we teach and model shared leadership to prevent our organizations from perpetuating the practice of having one leader at the head of the "V"?

2) How can we keep company with the fallen, supporting our colleagues and students when they're grounded, regardless of the reason?

3) How can we support those whom we follow, honking encouragement from behind and giving them inspiration so they can find the strength they need to reach collective goals?

The Role of Roles

"Magic mirror, won't you tell me please,

Do I see myself in anyone I meet?

Magic mirror, if we only could

Try to see ourselves as others really

would."

LEON RUSSELL

THERE'S nothing more difficult for some people — and I'm one of them — than role playing.

You know the drill: you're in a workshop and someone says, "Can I have a couple of volunteers for a little role playing?"

Right about then, I'm trying to become as small and inconspicuous as my weight and girth will allow. Maybe I've dropped my pen on the floor and I'm hunched over, acting like I'm trying to pick it up. If I've got a workbook for the presentation, I've just buried my face in it.

Some presenters, particularly those with killer instincts, look for people like me. They see it as their purpose in life to help "the rest of us" learn to overcome our shyness and step up to the plate.

I'm not shy. Far from it. I'm somewhat of a ham on my own terms. Trouble is, I prefer extemporaneous combustion. Give me the right scene, the right props, and a chance to play myself — and I'm *on*. My best material is unplanned, unscheduled, and unrehearsed. On the other hand, give me a role to play and I'm worse than most of your relatives on family videotapes.

Let the good times role.

Role playing can be an effective communication tool in the right hands, but I'm more interested in the roles we actually play in our organizations. What roles do you play? Don't confuse your role with your job, your responsibilities, or your functions. Your role — or roles — lie outside of the written descriptors of your formal assignment.

A role is not a function. Functions are specific assigned duties or activities associated with a position. Functions are generally associated with verbs such as advise, teach, supervise, train, direct, coordinate, prepare, report, plan, etc.

A role is not a position description. Position descriptions are documentation outlining responsibilities and duties (functions) as well as qualifications for a position. A position description could conceivably address roles, but it's not likely.

Roles are the acts or operations expected of a person — the socially expected behavior patterns determined by a person's status in a particular society. These expectations can come from above, below, or all around. Roles reflect the capacity or the position in which one functions within the group.

Leader. Stabilizer. Visionary. Analyzer. Cynic. Antagonist. Realist. Critic. Resolver. Agitator. Caretaker. Communicator.

Roles are influenced by personality. Different people bring different strengths and weaknesses with them; subsequently, the role of the position may change.

Different roles for different goals.

A few years ago, with my colleague Renee Staton, I examined organizational dynamics at the departmental level in a rapidly changing environment. We tried a new approach: looking at the organization through a perspective on roles rather than responsibilities. We had several questions: What types of roles do people play within the organization? Should roles be associated with job titles or levels? Can different people play different roles at different times? Do individuals within the organization perceive roles differently? Are some roles clandestine? What roles are required to most effectively meet organizational goals? (See *Organizational Stress: Studies in Role Conflict and Ambiguity*, by R.L. Kahn, D.M. Wolfe, R.P. Quinn, J.D. Snoek, and R.A. Rosenthal.)

We knew there were numerous lenses for assessing organizational effectiveness — organizational structure, achievement of departmental objectives, implementation of standards, utilization of position descriptions, student accomplishment on assorted instruments, etc. But we focused on examining roles, for several reasons.

First, traditional, formal approaches evaluated formal organization, not informal interaction; we wanted to tap into the informal dynamics of the organization. Second, staff members were unsure of their counterparts' roles and responsibilities due to rapid growth and expansion of services; we wanted to capture the essence of the organization in its metamorphosis. Third, the perceived roles of some positions seemed to conflict with specific job responsibilities; we wanted to help the organization redesign itself based on a clearer understanding of itself.

We started with a premise that roles affect communication and cooperation within the organization. We believed that roles, examined and understood, could help us become a more productive, effective organization. A scientific, quantitative study wasn't quite what we had in mind; it was more of an extended focus group, a self-study. We recognized that the success of our study was dependent upon group participation and cooperation. A strong antagonist (role) could adversely affect our outcomes — and sabotage was a distinct possibility.

Through a series of retreat activities, workshops, personal interviews, and follow-up discussions, we determined that there are at least three aspects to organizational roles:

1) *Ideal*: the imagined or preferred role to be played by an individual in a specific position or assignment. This is what others in the organization *desire*.

2) *Concealed*: covert roles, intentional or unintentional, that may affect the organization either positively (elves) or negatively (gremlins). This role is what others in the organization *suspect*.

3) *Real*: the role actually and visibly being played by the individual. This role is what others in the organization *see*.

Everyone's role was examined. The roles were then consolidated and captured to help emphasize the importance and value of each role. For instance, my role in the organization — I was director of the department at the time — was summarized as follows:

- **Ideal.** People in the organization desired a director who understood, encompassed, and represented the entire department; someone who "oversaw" the organization yet was also a hands-on initiator. Someone with guiding hands who wasn't afraid of getting them dirty. *Leader*.

- **Concealed.** People in the organization suspected that the director is caught between the needs of the organization and the greater needs of the institution. Someone who talks a good talk but walks the way the organizational wind blows. Someone who wears different hats and carries a big stick. *Boss*.

- **Real.** People in the organization saw the director as someone walking a daily tightrope. Someone who makes plans and sometimes has to change them. Someone who makes mistakes and sometimes makes amends. *Human*.

I saw myself as a composite of these three roles, with several others thrown in to meet specific circumstances. I wanted to be the leader, I frequently acted like the boss, and I always ended up being the human.

Ideally, our associate directors were supportive, resourceful "stand-ins" for the director. Their concealed role was that of a barrier, a gatekeeper for the director, an extra layer of management and decision making. Realistically, they were people trying to bridge the departmental units without compromising the needs of the units or the department, not unlike the role the director played in the larger division.

Ideally, our assistant directors and coordinators were managers who worked closely with students to oversee an area or specific projects within an area. Their concealed role was that of conduit or messenger, passing down directions or orders from above. Realistically, they were people responsible for coordinating complex assignments with limited resources in a changing environment.

Ideally, our technicians and administrative assistants provided support, handled the details, and held the department together. Their concealed role was that of underling or functionary, someone's right hand, the frontline soldiers resistant to change. Realistically, they were people who provided support, handled the details, and held the department together. In this category, the real and the ideal were relatively close.

Our real and ideal roles suggested connectedness and networks; our concealed roles suggested a traditional, hierarchical, pyramid structure. Could we, through a better understanding of roles, change the organization to be more real and ideal? Could we put to rest some of our unrealistic expectations about people and positions?

Could we reveal the concealed and make the ideal real?

For example, some staff members perceived the associate directors as unnecessary and unable to adequately serve as resources or supervisors (real). Some staff members believed that the associate directors were consciously or unconsciously sabotaging the efforts of other staff (concealed). Some staff members believed that the associate directors should be responsible for building relationships and promoting the philosophy and mission of the department, both internally and externally (ideal). The subsequent changes in the associate directors' responsibilities — particularly the creation of a higher level of support rather than an additional level of supervision — reflect the incorporation of the ideal characteristics into the associate director's role.

What types of roles — ideal, concealed, and real — do people play within your organization? Figure out which is which and you're well on your way to improving the organization.

By identifying and understanding what people perceive to be the real and ideal roles in the organization, a group can ascertain where they are and where they want to go in terms of training and professional development (*who are we now and who do we want to be?*). The desirable components of an integrated organization can be inventoried, and new staff can be selected in part to help fill the vacant *roles* in the organization, not just the vacant *positions*.

By identifying and understanding what people perceive to be the concealed roles in the organization, a group can collectively work to minimize the negative effects of hierarchy, power, and competition. And some of the group's unrealistic expectations and incorrect assumptions can be put to rest.

Reveal the concealed and make the ideal real.

Should roles be associated with job titles or levels? Ideally, no. Realistically, yes. Understanding what the organization needs at a particular level is critical to success at that level.

Can different people play different roles at different times? It's required. A role is essentially a reaction.

Do individuals within the organization perceive roles differently? Undoubtedly, particularly when it comes to the concealed roles. Find out what people really see and what they really desire.

Are some roles clandestine? Yes. Elves and gremlins exist in many forms. If possible, surround yourself with elves. And don't give the gremlins water after midnight.

What roles are required to most effectively meet organizational goals? It depends on the organization. It doesn't hurt to have leaders and followers, a few stabilizers, some visionaries and analyzers, quite a few communicators — even a few realists and critics. What roles does your organization need?

REFLECTION

1) In your organization, what would people say are your ideal, concealed, and real roles?

2) Could you, through a better understanding of roles, change your organization to be more real and ideal? If so, how?

3) What are some circumstances in which your role would need to change?

HVAC 101

"The river can be hot or cold,

And you should dive right into it,

Else you'll find

It's passed you by."

DAVID CROSBY

Magic Days

MID June. Hazy. Hot. Humid. It's one of those years when winter stayed too long, spring never came, and summer arrived with a vengeance. Thunderstorm weather.

My current office has a window unit air conditioner. The noise can be distracting, but it's too hot to turn off the AC. Opening the windows would only let in the humidity. It's a blessing to finally have an office with operable windows, but today that's a moot point. For now, I'll "suffer" the noise of the machine and enjoy its cool breezes.

If your campus is like mine, it's likely that heating and air conditioning are ruled by "magic days." The decision to turn on the heat or the air conditioning is determined by the calendar, not by the weather.

"It's November 15; time to turn on the heat."

It doesn't matter if it's 75 degrees on November 15, or if there's been snow on the ground since the middle of September. November 15 is the magic day when the heat comes on.

"It's April 15; time to turn on the air conditioning."

We've been sweating bullets since the beginning of March, but April 15 is the magic day. Even if there's ice forming on the corners of the windows, when April 15 comes, we turn on the air conditioning.

We've always done it that way.

Budget? Perhaps. Technology? Not anymore. Tradition? Probably.

And who's in charge of this annual process? It's our old friend, the physical plant manager.

"It's the Chiller"

I once heard a characterization of the physical plant manager for a nearby campus. He sounded familiar; maybe you've met him. He was an older man, frequently seen with a lit cigar (Sir Walter Raleigh owes all of us an apology for that particular innovation). He generally had an opinion on just about everything unrelated to physical plant administration (and he was happy to share it with you). And no matter what went wrong with a building, he seemed to have the same tired, time-tested refrain ...

"The chiller's down."

Your phones don't work? The chiller's down. No lights in your office? It's the chiller. Too much heat or not enough? You got it: the chiller. Air conditioning on the fritz? Repeat after me: it's the chiller. Doors and windows won't open; funny smells in the corridor; locks that won't turn. You name it, the chiller's down.

The crazy part of all of this was that people believed it! Since most people don't know what a chiller is or what it does, they took the man's word that all of their mechanical and facilities problems could be blamed on one mysterious hunk of metal, plumbing, and wiring.

Wouldn't it be great if all of us in higher education had a chiller to blame when things weren't working the way we wished?

"Why can't your people get reports in on time?" ("The chiller's down.")

"You've gone over budget again!" (Couldn't be helped; it was the chiller's fault.")

"No one seems to be taking responsibility for effective communication." ("It's no wonder, the way that chiller is working.")

No, we don't have the luxury of blaming our shortcomings or limitations on a box. Well, maybe we do. We could substitute the "chiller" of the 1990s ...

The computer!

I hear that most chillers now are actually managed by computers. If that physical plant manager ever retires, I wonder how I would go about getting his job ...

People Conditioning

The problem isn't really with the equipment at all; it's with the people who operate it, use it, and complain about it when it isn't just right. It's almost impossible to set the temperature in a room at a level that is satisfactory to more than one person (and it's sometimes a challenge getting it right for that one person). One degree lower and people are running for their sweaters and jackets. One degree higher and beads of sweat appear. The larger the room, the greater the capacity for disagreement about the temperature.

If you've ever been in any kind of a relationship at all, you've already learned that there is no compatibility when it comes to temperature. One is wrapped in flannel pajamas, sheets, blankets, comforters, and quilts; the other prefers a minimum of clothing, no blankets, and an open window. How many good relationships have ended through the misunderstanding of temperature diversity? It's no use to tell your partner that the chiller's down.

Warmth and comfort are relative; it's time we learned that.

Have you ever noticed that the people who are the least tolerant of temperature changes are always assigned to work in areas where the heating and air conditioning are problematic? A coincidence? I don't think so.

Who got the idea in the last half of this century to design buildings with inoperable windows? It took centuries for the human race to develop windows that could be opened and closed on demand; it took a decade or two to throw all of this innovation out the window, so to speak. What were we thinking?

Many people confuse air conditioning with temperature control. That's only part of the equation. To be effective, air conditioning has to deal with humidity. Too much or not enough causes problems. To be effective, air conditioning has to deal with ventilation and air exchange. All of the air in the room has to be turned over in a reasonable amount of time.

Temperature, humidity, and ventilation: they're all factors in air conditioning.

If it's impossible to adjust the air conditioning to everyone's satisfaction, perhaps we should try "people conditioning."

People conditioning implies adjusting to the highs and lows of your life. It implies taking responsibility for attitudes, emotions, and reactions — making your own weather (and not blaming the chiller ...). It implies determining each day to be a magic day, heating up or cooling down as necessary, not waiting for the calendar or someone else to make that decision for you. It implies exchanging the bad air for good air on a regular basis. Temperature, "humility," and ventilation: they're all factors in people conditioning.

One last aspect of air conditioning worth sharing is the notion of positive and negative pressure. Picture yourself in an air-conditioned room. If you open the door and a blast of hotter air comes flooding in from outside, you've got negative pressure. If you're outside this room, open the door, and feel a blast of cool air, that's positive pressure. The same applies to heat. Positive pressure keeps the room close to the desired temperature; negative pressure means the room temperature is subject to fluctuation when the door opens. In other words, positive pressure is desirable.

Positive and negative pressure apply to people conditioning as well. If you open up your door (metaphorically speaking) and you're blasted by outside forces, chances are you're suffering from negative pressure. If, on the other hand, someone else opens up your door and feels your presence and energy flowing out, that's positive pressure. Positive pressure is desirable.

You have a choice. You can emulate the physical plant manager and blame whatever *chiller* happens to be handy, or you can make the necessary adjustments in your work and in your life. You can hold out for arbitrary *magic days* to make significant changes, or you can learn to make every day a magic day with your *positive pressure*. You can focus on trying to make everyone happy through periodic adjustments to morale, or you can focus on your daily interpersonal interactions and see how many BTUs of *people conditioning* you can generate.

REFLECTION

1) How could you use the notion of "people conditioning" to examine problems with your staff?

2) Do you have any magic days that might be seen as arbitrary by your students, co-workers, or peers? If so, what can you do to change that?

3) What's your "chiller"?

Treasures

"Value is impossible to measure;

People find their treasures where they will."

R.L.M.

IN fairy tales and pirate stories, treasures were often critical story elements. Dashing heroes and ravishing heroines set off on impossible quests to protect, discover, or reclaim something of value. The quest was frequently more important than the illusive treasure; the treasure often turned out to be something altogether different than was originally imagined.

Treasures are sometimes lost, sometimes found, sometimes imaginary, sometimes real. They have no inherent value unless they're shared and examined. They have no worth unless someone wants or needs them.

A treasure's only priceless when it doesn't have a price.

Many years ago, I was told the legend of Ali Hafad, a Persian who dreamed of the great diamond discoveries in South Africa. Though he was, by most standards, already a wealthy man, Ali Hafad was enticed to leave his family and his home in search of extravagant wealth and the allure of the diamonds.

Selling some of his property to finance his journey, Ali Hafad bid his wife and children a hasty farewell and set off for distant lands and the promise of fortune. He wandered through the wilds of Africa for many years, never to find an unclaimed deposit of the precious stones. Ali Hafad died a poor and tired man, leagues away from his home. His family had long since scattered, and his property, once rich and productive, lay in waste.

Some fifty years after his death, the richest deposit of diamonds ever discovered in the Middle East, including the famed Hope Diamond, was unearthed on the property that once belonged to Ali Hafad.

Dorothy was right (and Toto too!).

The quest was frequently more important than the illusive treasure; the treasure often turned out to be something altogether different than was originally imagined.

> *"... if my treasures were collected*
> *in a room with locks and keys*
>
> *they'd escape inside a memory*
> *to treasure when I please*
>
> *for the madness of the moneyman,*
> *you might as well throw dice*
>
> *a treasure's only priceless when it*
> *doesn't have a price ..."*

There's a storefront tavern about a half-block from the only stoplight in an indistinguishable Front Range town in central Colorado. The owner, a retired shoe retailer wanting something to do with his spare time and savings, converted his shoe store into a bar, where he spent his nights serving 3)2 beer and frozen pizzas to the recently graduated farm kids, none of whom were college bound. Out of their boredom and sweat, out of their menial jobs and broken high school romances, they came on Wednesday night to hear the Clay Pigeons, a rock and roll/country band imported from the city ...

We were gonna be rich and famous someday; or so we told the people who came to hear us play. And in between the stolen jokes and the rum-and-cokes and the backstage smokes, we sang about the things we didn't have the guts to say.

Eightball for a quarter. Jukebox for a dime. Tell me where we lost control of time.

We were looking for passion in the night, because the darkness always looks better in the light. We sang about the beauty queens and the Maybellines in tight blue jeans, and acted out the parts in songs that we would later write.

Can I have the next dance? Can I take you home? No one wants to spend the night alone.

Value is impossible to measure; people find their treasures where they will. But some of the best times I ever had to kill, were shooting the bull and a little pool in the Alley Bar and Grill.

We were gonna be rich and famous someday, but somehow working for a living got in the way. We settled down to live our lives in our eight-to-fives with our kids and wives, and acted out the parts in songs that we would never play.

Maybe there's a memory, waiting for us still, somewhere in the Alley Bar and Grill.

Looking back — way back — I see myself on the stage with one of my guitars, having just passed my master's degree oral exam earlier in the day, with the inevitable postpartum depression setting in. I was married, I was educated, and I had a few job prospects in faraway places. What the hell was I doing in the Alley Bar and Grill? I was torn between two worlds: responsible adulthood and the never-ending freedom of extended adolescence. With the gentlest of shoves I could go either way.

That night, the music sounded better to me than it ever had. The blues were meaner; the rockers were rowdier; the slow songs were sweeter; the harmonies were tighter. That night, I sang my heart out because it was breaking anyway. Old hearts need to break so new hearts can grow.

The music was loud, the natives were restless, and the beer was cold. I guess *value is impossible to measure; people find their treasures where they will. But some of the best times I've ever had to kill were shooting the bull and a little pool in the Alley Bar and Grill.*

The quest was frequently more important than the illusive treasure; the treasure often turned out to be something altogether different than was originally imagined.

———◦•◦———

Have you ever found a treasure? It doesn't have to be worth a lot of money. The greater the extrinsic value, the less its intrinsic value. Value is impossible to measure; people find their treasures where they will.

We're participants in a great treasure hunt called higher education. The treasures are there for anyone to claim. Knowledge. Wisdom. Competency. Opportunity. Understanding. Compassion. Beauty. Truth. The treasures are just below the surface, but you have to know where to dig and you have to keep trying when you fail to find them. The treasures are sometimes lost, sometimes found, sometimes imaginary, sometimes real. They have no inherent value unless they're shared and examined. They have no worth unless someone wants or needs them.

A treasure's only priceless when it doesn't have a price.

Graduate school. The job search. Making the first professional presentation or submitting that first manuscript. Seeking new responsibilities. Starting construction or renovation projects. Inaugurating a program. Learning from mistakes. Hiring staff. Moving to a different institution. Creating a curriculum. Serving in a leadership capacity. The quest is frequently more important than the illusive treasure: the treasure often turns out to be something altogether different than was originally imagined.

Value is impossible to measure; people find their treasures where they will.

REFLECTION

1) What treasures do you seek in higher education, either as a worker in higher education, a person pursuing a degree in higher education, or both?

2) How are you pursuing these treasures?

3) Are your treasures somewhere off in the distance, or in your proverbial back yard?

Cultural Distinction (What's My Culture?)

"Can you see the real me,

Can you?"

PETE TOWNSEND

CULTURE'S a tough egg to crack. I've seen many talented people try and fail.

Ismail, a colleague of mine, seems to have an approach that works well with student and staff groups. I've borrowed his activity many times (as I'm sure he borrowed it from someone else). Perhaps it will work for you as well.

First, you ask the group you're working with to help you define culture. Using a marker board or flip chart, you ask the group members to come up with as many aspects of culture as they can. What do we mean by culture? What distinguishes one culture from another? Are there words, phrases, or practices that define culture? What is culture?

The group then begins to offer suggestions. Clothing. Food. Religion. Music. Family relations. Emphasis on age or youth. Roles for women, men, and children. Traditions, holidays, and rituals. Perspectives on time. Region of birth or upbringing. Values. Taboos. Emphasis on different types of learning. Responses to health. The list goes on, depending on the sophistication and experience of the group.

I've seen this activity conducted several times. Rarely is the word "race" included in the list. When it is, it's one of fifteen to twenty considerations, not the solitary consideration in defining culture. My friend Ismail makes a stronger point. He says that the combination of aspects that make up the list — and not race or skin color alone — defines culture. He adds: "I didn't wake up this morning and say, 'I'm black this morning, by noon I'll be even blacker, and by tonight I'll be so black I won't know what to do with myself!'" Rather, he concentrates on what he's going to wear that day. He anticipates the meals he'll enjoy, depending on the day. He might be thinking about a religious activity or family activity in which he'll participate. These are the things that, to him, define his culture.

Labeling people under the heading of just one culture is next to impossible. Case in point: I'm a white male, born in 1954 in a semi-suburban community in Colorado. I have an older brother and two younger sisters, one who is gay. Both of my parents were married more than once. Their parents, as children, "pioneered" to western Nebraska and eastern Colorado at the turn of the century. Ancestral names like Yates, Hickman, McCormack, and Mitchell are readily traced to the British Isles. I was raised in a fundamentalist Christian church but have been involved in Unitarian and Brethren churches over the past twenty years. I'm married (over twenty years) with children, but I rarely see my siblings or in-laws. I normally vote for individuals, not parties. A first-generation college student, I went on to earn a master's degree and complete some work at the doctoral level. I work in higher education so I'll never be rich, but I make a comfortable living. I'm in a two-income marriage. I've lived in the suburban West, the urban Southeast, and the rural Atlantic seaboard. I'm overweight, experience kidney stones on a regular basis, and take medications for digestion. I like to cook Mexican dishes, and my favorite restaurant is Mexican (no connection to the previous sentence …). I dress conservatively for work but prefer shorts and T-shirts when I'm home. I listen to classic rock, classical, and New Age music, but I used to play in a jazz combo. This is probably more than you ever wanted to know about me.

What's my culture?

There are numerous other white males in my age group who wouldn't identify with me, my choices, my beliefs, or my practices — nor I with theirs. Do I share a culture with them? Is culture a perception or a perspective? Whose — mine or those who categorize me?

We have a problem. We jump to cultural conclusions.

If your skin is a certain color, you like certain types of music.

If you grew up in a specific region, you eat certain types of foods.

If you belong to a certain religious order, you believe certain things.

If you're a member of a designated ethnic group, you'll respond to authority in an expected manner.

If you come from certain countries, you'll have strong opinions on gender roles.

As long as we try to be armchair anthropologists, we're going to be wrong more often than we're right.

I don't have a handle on culture, primarily because I don't think there is any such thing as pure culture. I believe most people in our society are products of numerous, simultaneous cultural influences. If you ask everyone you know to do a thumbnail biographical sketch as I've done above, you'll begin to see the diversity of influences affecting those around you. Diversity within cultures as we've defined them is often more dynamic and meaningful than is the diversity between and among cultures.

If our efforts in diversity training are directed toward getting students and staff to better understand culture, we might make some progress — but not enough. "A little knowledge is a dangerous thing," Alexander Pope pointed out several hundred years ago. We've only taught our students and staff to label and categorize others, not to understand them. Putting people in cultural boxes is a dead end.

We need to learn to see individuals as culturally distinct, just as they are genetically distinct. Understanding biology, chemistry, psychology, and sociology helps us understand the quality of being human, but these disciplines don't tell us the story of the individual; this can only be experienced personally. The same is true with culture. We should develop cultural competency (awareness, attitudes, knowledge, skills) so that we have a better understanding of cultural influences, but this understanding is relevant only in the context of the individual with whom we're engaging. The individual is not the culture, nor does culture define the individual. Culture is one of many influences, and individuals are influenced by multiple cultures. These multiple cultures, not unlike the multiple relationships held by the individual, shape but do not make the individual.

We're all culturally and genetically distinct.

Don't get me wrong. Recognition and appreciation of culture are incredibly important. Everyone has a bit of heritage that, like their name, helps to identify them. We need to acknowledge and celebrate this heritage – and then go beyond and beneath it to appreciate the individual wearing the name and the culture. We need to get to know the individual through his or her beliefs, values, experiences, accomplishments, relationships, and personal history. We can't assume we're capable of categorizing or labeling anyone effectively. Instead, we should learn to listen and listen to learn. We must apologize if we step on any toes, then respectfully ask questions for clarification. We can strive to build a better relationship; "seek first to understand" the person, not the demographic or ethnic classification to which he or she might belong.

Some of my professional colleagues are assimilationists. They believe diversity is a threat to societal unity. They examine cultures as different, conflicting entities in need of assimilation into the greater society. Unfortunately, the cost of unity at this level is all too frequently oppression. This perspective is uni-cultural, ignoring the possibilities and the value of multiple perspectives. In this line of reasoning, the sooner "others" adapt to the majority culture, the sooner they will be able to successfully participate in that culture.

Some of my professional colleagues are cultural pluralists. They believe diversity is a higher principle than societal unity. They examine cultures as isolated, autonomous entities, self-defined, somewhat absolute and static. Unfortunately, the cost of diversity at this level is all too frequently social disintegration. This is a plural-cultural perspective, ignoring the interconnectedness and multiple influences of cultures on one another. Plural ethnocentrism (many isolated entities) results in boundaries, barriers, and internecine strife.

Some of my professional colleagues are multiculturalists. They believe diversity is an important consideration in creating societal unity. They examine cultures as connected, overlapping entities, defined as much by outside influences as by inside considerations. To fully understand a culture, one must understand the other cultures that interact with that culture. This is a multi-cultural perspective, exploring relationships between and among individuals and groups. Multiculturalists come closer to understanding the multiple influences that affect not only groups of people, but also the individuals who make up those groups. (See "Cultural Diversity or Diverse Cultures: The Tangled 'Foliage' of Multiculturalism," by R.D. Manning, *Proteus: A Journal of Ideas*, Vol. 10, No. 1, Spring 1993, pp. 3-10.)

Treating people with cultural distinction isn't easy. (The only thing that's easy about cultural distinction is our capacity to make mistakes.) Our biases, prejudices, assumptions, and beliefs have deep roots, thanks to our parents, our schools, our churches, our friends, our media, and our own limited perspectives on the complex human condition. To successfully understand and interact with the increasing diversity inherent in our changing student bodies, we as student affairs professionals must branch out from our roots. Cultural distinction implies that we must recognize each student as an individual of inherent worth and dignity, greater than the confines of any given culture. A multicultural view is more likely to result in the recognition of cultural distinction.

Ask your students individually, "What's your culture?" Listen for and treat them with distinction. Like fingerprints, no two are exactly alike. And after you've asked your students where they came from, be sure to ask them where they're going.

Ask yourself, "What's my culture?" Listen for and treat yourself with distinction.

REFLECTION

1) What are some examples of programs or services you have experienced that were successful in developing multicultural skills, knowledge, or attitudes on the part of students or staff? Why did they work? What are some examples that were unsuccessful? Why?

2) What attitudes, awareness, skills, and knowledge do student affairs professionals need that are related to cultural competency?

3) How would you determine someone's cultural distinction?

Transition

"And these children that you spit on
As they try to change their worlds
Are immune to your consolations
They're quite aware of what they're
going through."

DAVID BOWIE

I'VE become one of *them*. You know who *we* are; you see *us* each summer or fall, as faithfully as the changing seasons. We all look different, yet we have something in common, something special. You know of whom I speak.

We're the parents of college students.

My oldest daughter just graduated from high school. She's filled with hopes, dreams, fears, and expectations of what lies ahead, and she's college bound. She's strong and fragile; grown up and growing; courageous and anxious; beautiful and seeking beauty; honest and seeking the truth; wise with still so much to learn.

She's coming our way.

For nineteen years I've seen students just like her go through orientation and enter college in the fall. I didn't recognize her, but she was there. She was someone's daughter or son; someone's husband or wife; someone's grandchild; someone's pride and joy. She was — and is — someone's past, present, and future. She was — and is — someone special.

She's coming our way.

It would be easy to just think of her as an enrollment, a social security number, a file folder, a name on a checklist, a statistic. That's exactly how many students appear to far too many of us in higher education. It would be easy to lose her in the policies, procedures, rules, and regulations that we spell out so carefully in our handbooks and catalogs. It would be easy to label her as a freshman, a first-year student, an English major, a Caucasian female, an in-state student, a work-study student, a transfer student, a sorority sister, a customer or a consumer — *but she's so much more than that!*

She's coming our way.

If you're employed by the college where my daughter enrolls, here are my requests.

Pretend she's your daughter, or the daughter of a friend or relative, or, at the very least, someone you care about.

Don't think of her as a student. Think of her as a young adult who's engaged in learning.

See her as a rare flower to cultivate, not a dandelion to weed out. Assume she will succeed.

Create an environment in which learning is the most important expectation, and assess the effectiveness of that environment.

When she has a problem, assume it's as important as whatever you were working on before she brought it to your attention.

Remove as many artificial obstacles to her learning and development as you can; she'll take care of the rest.

Assist her through her transitions into, through, and out of the college experience. Assume she will succeed.

She's coming our way.

In the film *Phenomenon,* John Travolta's character is forced to help a young child understand the concept of death. Using an apple, he explains to the child that we can enjoy the beauty, nutrition, and flavor of the apple, or we can throw it on the ground and let it rot. He concludes by telling the child that everything is on its way to another place. In other words, *carpe diem.* In other words, gather ye rosebuds while ye may. In other words, an eloquent metaphor for transition.

College is a time of transition for all students, regardless of their age, gender, ethnicity, previous experience, or interests. Unfortunately, the perception is growing, particularly among the parents of college students and certain legislators, that the primary goal of higher education should be getting jobs rather than getting educated. Far too many students — and the people who pay their bills — think getting through college quickly is more important than taking an extra semester to learn what they need to survive and thrive in a changing world. With a focus on meeting minimum expectations rather than maximizing potential, the ability of higher education to develop human capital is diminished.

Fortunately, not everyone subscribes to these notions.

People in higher education have recently begun to talk seriously of student success. Simply stated, student success involves designing, implementing, managing, and assessing learning opportunities that help students complete seamless transitions into, through, and out of college. Students who successfully complete these transitions will reach desired levels of academic achievement and career, personal, and leadership development.

Student success is ultimately a matter of successful transition. Students must successfully negotiate a series of *transitions* into, through, and out of the university.

First, the student encounters the *entering* transition: orientation to the institution's expectations and resources; matriculation into the academic program; assimilation into the student body.

Second, the student undergoes the *planning* transition: making informed decisions about academic majors, careers, values, and involvement; making progress through the college experience.

Finally, the student experiences the *culminating* transition: successful passage to graduate or professional school, post-college work, and full citizenship in their chosen communities. To help students successfully complete these transitions, higher education can develop learning opportunities, formerly referred to as programs and services but with a renewed focus on learning outcomes. To develop learning opportunities directly related to each of the transitions listed above, I offer a tool developed by the student success team with which I work. The acronym for this tool is SCORE: skills, community, obstacles, resources, and expectations. For each transition, ask the following questions:

- What *skills* must the student develop to successfully complete this transition?

- How does the institution assist the student in becoming or remaining a member of the campus *community* during this transition? (And in the final transition, how does the institution assist the student in becoming a citizen-leader in the larger community?)

- What are the *obstacles* the student must overcome during this transition?

- What *resources* does the institution direct toward the students who are in the midst of this transition?

- What are the institution's *expectations* of the student during this transition?

To apply this model, think for a moment about the new students entering the institution. What skills do they need, right away, to successfully make the transition? Self-reliance? Study skills? Time management? How can these skills be addressed through orientation, residence life programs, and other efforts? How can these skills be front-loaded? Without adequate skills, student success is by default rather than by design.

Next, how does the student truly become — and remain — a member of the campus community in an effort to successfully complete an academic program? What ceremonies, rituals, activities, involvement, and interventions lead to community? How do we keep students from falling through the cracks? How do we expose students to the wonders and possibilities of diversity? What is a learning community? What learning opportunities lead to these discoveries? If students don't become effective members of the community, student success is by default rather than by design.

All students face obstacles to their success: academic integrity and honor violations, alcohol and substance abuse, relationship issues, financial difficulties, pathologies, and an ever-growing list of unexpected barriers. How do we point these barriers out to students, and what can we do to help students overcome them? If we don't help students address obstacles, student success is by default rather than by design.

Colleges and universities generally have resources set aside to assist students in achieving academic and personal success. What are these resources? How visible and accessible are they? Are students, their faculty, and their advisors aware of the many programs and services available to them? How integrated and cooperative are these resources? Without effective utilization of available resources, student success is by default rather than by design.

Though we print policies, procedures, rules, and regulations in our student handbooks and catalogs, we rarely *talk* about the expectations higher education has of the student. What does your institution expect of the student, academically and experientially, and why? What are the consequences if these expectations aren't met? If the student doesn't clearly understand these expectations, student success is by default rather than by design.

Student success has to be an *institutional* consideration. Student success is best facilitated when the institution as a whole celebrates learning as the primary institutional purpose, directs appropriate resources toward the accomplishment of learning, and expects everyone at the institution to cross organizational boundaries in the pursuit of learning. Student success requires creating conditions that motivate and inspire students to learn; student success requires removing barriers to learning. (See Wingspread Group on Higher Education [1993], *An American Imperative: Higher Expectations for Higher Education*, The Johnson Foundation, Inc.)

Student success has to be a *departmental* consideration. Student success requires designing, implementing, managing, and assessing learning opportunities that help students complete seamless transitions. Student success requires faculty and staff partnership. Student success requires creating common, shared experiences and rituals that generate a sense of community for the students. Student success requires making the first year — for both freshman and transfer students — an institutional priority. (See Barefoot, B., & Fidler, P. [1996], *The 1994 National Survey of Freshman Seminar Programs: Continuing Innovations in the Collegiate Curriculum* [Monograph No. 20], National Resource Center for the Freshman Year Experience and Students in Transition, University of South Carolina.)

Finally, student success has to be a *personal* consideration. Student success requires our individual efforts to help students understand that success is not a matter of starting salaries and material possessions; rather, it is a quality of character, illustrated long ago by Ralph Waldo Emerson:

> *"… [T]o appreciate beauty; to find the best in others;*
> *to give of one's self; to leave the world a bit better …*
> *to know even one life has breathed easier because*
> *you have lived — this is to have succeeded."*

Student success requires professionals in student affairs to ask these questions every day, and to assess for every student: "What does this student need?" and "How can I help him or her succeed?" Student success requires us to remove as many artificial obstacles to student learning and development as we can, knowing that the student will take care of the rest. Student success requires a commitment from all of us to see each student as someone special: someone's daughter or son, worth every bit of our attention and focus. Student success requires *us* to assume that *they* will succeed.

They're coming our way.

REFLECTION

1) What role does your department play in transition and student success?
   What, specifically, is your role?

2) How do you collaborate with others to achieve student success?
   How might you collaborate more effectively?

3) What are your institution's weaknesses in transition and student success, and how would you, as a parent, expect the institution to address those weaknesses to benefit your daughter or son?

Old Soldiers

"Old soldiers don't die,

They just fade away

Like the endings to songs

That they borrow to play."

R.L.M.

"STORMIN' Norman" we called him, our musical mentor and bandleader. Norm was in his early forties, with slightly graying hair and the beginnings of a paunch. He was an Old Soldier, our term for the bandleaders and musicians who never quite made it into the big time. Long before the term was used to describe a national figure in a war we could never have imagined, Stormin' Norman was a minor league legend, a weekend warrior in the part-time musicians militia. With stacks and stacks of fake books, charts for the latest Top 40 hits, and a repertoire of oldies and standards unlike any I'd ever seen, Stormin' Norman commanded his corner of the globe.

"He's been on the road for so long,

He's forgotten the words to the song,

So he makes them up and they come out wrong

Old Soldiers, standing in line."

Butch and I were nineteen-year-old college sophomores in need of spending money and something to do on weekend nights. We dreamed of being the next big thing in popular music, greeting each other with the refrain, "Are we rich and famous yet?"

Butch doubled on drums and guitar, adding harmonies where required. I played bass guitar and a little rhythm and sang lead. Stormin' Norman played the keyboards. We hooked up with Norm in the Normandy House Trio, a combination of parts of our names, to play the Holiday Inn and country club circuit of Northern Colorado, Western Nebraska, and Southern Wyoming.

> *"Once, long ago, he was young,*
>
> *And the music just rolled off his tongue*
>
> *And everyone knew all the songs he had sung*
>
> *Old Soldiers, marching in time."*

Norm had been playing in similar ensembles for over twenty years, cultivating young apprentices like ourselves and teaching them the tricks of the trade in the middle-of-the-road dance hall business, always losing his young recruits when they outgrew his musical vision. Yet Stormin' Norman kept on playing. We could never figure out what motivated him: the music or the opportunity to escape an unpleasant home life. Stormin' Norman kept on playing the same old songs to the same old faces. He took few chances and kept the tunes light, upbeat, danceable, and familiar. We wanted to play the music that we liked; Norm insisted we play the music that the audience wanted.

> *"He knew all the changes,*
> *but never could make them;*
>
> *He knew all the odds,*
> *but let someone else take them.*
>
> *He lived for the sound of the scattered applause;*
>
> *He knew the effects, but he didn't know the cause."*

Eventually, Butch and I followed our own dreams of music, education, and employment. I moved to another state to begin a career in higher education. Butch opened a music store in a small town outside of Denver. Occasionally, I traveled back to Colorado and found opportunities to sit in with whatever incarnation of a band Butch was heading at the time. I lost track of Stormin' Norman but heard he still played solo or in jazz trios in small clubs across the western prairie.

> *"The one-nights in Holiday Inns*
>
> *The bar drinks and overnight sins*
>
> *The battle with time that nobody wins*
>
> *Old Soldiers, standing alone."*

Many years later, I visited Butch and agreed to sit in on one of his gigs. With Butch at the wheel and a college freshman drummer in the back of the van, a curious thought came to mind: Did we look the same to the kid in the back as Norm had to us years before? Were we the new generation of Old Soldiers, the hacks that kept on playing, breaking in the rookies as they laughed behind our backs, swearing to never end up like us?

That revelation was over ten years ago. I've long since retired from the weekend warrior school of music, realizing — in the words of Harry Chapin — that music was a part of my life, not my livelihood. Raising a family, building a career, engaging in community activities — numerous distractions get in the way of our simple dreams. Butch and I never got rich and famous, but we had some good times on and off the stage.

> *"But the stage lights have faded to black,*
>
> *And the regulars aren't coming back;*
>
> *He's one step behind, unaware of the fact.*
>
> *Old Soldiers, longing for home."*

I went through several stages of appreciation for Stormin' Norman. In stage one, I idolized him. I'd never met anyone as well-educated, self-assured, and competent as Norm. No one taught me more, inside or outside the classroom, than Norm. He became my academic advisor as well as my musical mentor; he guided me through the transitions of college and beyond and no doubt influenced my interest in a higher education career.

When I outgrew Norm's tutelage — stage two — I rejected his vision, as apprentices are apt to do. One generation removed, I had to dance and sing to the tune of another drummer (Butch notwithstanding), and our separation was rocky, not unlike that of a father and son. At the time, Norm appeared stodgy, aging, out of touch. I left his nest to create my own.

In retrospect — stage three — I began to see Norm as he really was: fundamentally flawed yet resourceful, creative, enthusiastic, and authentic. Teaching was his life, whether in the classroom or on the stage. I was but one of many interns lucky enough to study under Stormin' Norman. An Old Soldier? Perhaps. But he was also a survivor.

He taught me that you could never do your best — conduct research, play an instrument, make love, or use any of your senses — under the influence of alcohol or other drugs. He taught me to consider the audience when you're teaching a class, writing an article, or playing a song. He taught me that educational disciplines are interrelated: music is math is language is logic. He taught me that critical thinking is one of the greatest gifts found through higher education. He taught me to find my own voice.

Somewhere tonight, in a nondescript lounge in Northern Colorado, I have a feeling that Stormin' Norman is still playing those old songs. I hope he has a college student or two in his entourage.

I've come to realize that Old Soldiers come in many forms — stage four — perhaps to be found in every profession. You can recognize them in every professional organization, and they're frequently visible at professional conferences. You can find them on every campus. Call them mentors if you like. Call them old farts if you must. But don't hesitate to call them if you need a little wisdom added to your knowledge.

I used to be disrespectful of the Old Soldiers in my profession. I laughed at their ceremonies and rituals, disdained their cigar-clouded head tables, demeaned their inside jokes, and vowed to never end up like them. It took me years to finally see these folks in terms of the third and fourth stages of appreciation that I have described. They've fought their battles on various battlegrounds, winning some and losing some. In their tours of duty, they've experienced casualties I may have yet to face. They've seen recruits come and go. They've earned their stripes — or not — and they've carried on. They too are survivors.

As we become Old Soldiers — it's inevitable unless we change careers, win the lottery, or die — we have endless opportunities to go above and beyond the call of duty. We can use our cumulative knowledge, competence, and experience to train new recruits as they make their transitions into, through, and out of the profession. We can dedicate ourselves to guiding students through their transitions into, through, and out of the college experience.

Like Stormin' Norman, we can make lasting impressions on those who wind up serving with us — though they, like me, may not realize it for years to come.

REFLECTION

1) Who are some of the Old Soldiers that have influenced your development, and what have they taught you?

2) How have you (or have you?) gone through the stages of appreciation for your Old Soldiers?

3) Are you now, or do you anticipate becoming, an Old Soldier?
   Why or why not?

The Ethics of Political Correctness

"Now with the wisdom of years

I try to reason things out

And the only people I fear

Are those who never have doubts."

BILLY JOEL

YEARS ago, I was asked to sit on a panel for a presentation at an international conference. This panel was to identify a group of "established" professionals in the field and have them address questions concerning contemporary issues, but without the benefit of preparation. In effect, put some people on the spot, ask them tough questions, and then see what type of discussion is stimulated by their replies.

The panel was relatively diverse, with both sexes evenly represented and with a good mix of ethnic backgrounds. Various types of campuses were represented, from urban community colleges to large research institutions. The questions covered the spectrum of timely issues: unionization on campus; equity pay; alcohol and other drug abuse; liability.

I remember my question well:

"What's politically correct on your campus?"

The term had recently come into our collective language, though it had not yet elicited the backlash that would come from within and beyond the campus. At the moment in question, it had only a positive connotation. From what I could tell, it meant that you were up to date with a primarily liberal political agenda and that this was the "correct" agenda to promote.

Although I considered myself at the time to be on the liberal side of the political arena – socially, spiritually, and fiscally – the question and its implications bothered me. In my campus role, I had learned to work with all students from all political perspectives, from the radicals on the left and right to all of the student groups and causes that fell in between. Student development had to come from a position of tolerance and appreciation, not preference. I gave equal time to the Young Democrats, the College Republicans, and the various spin-offs of these groups who felt that their originators didn't lean far enough to the left or right. I considered the needs of the pro-life student groups to be as important as those of the pro-choice groups. It was not my position or place on the campus to promote an agenda that diminished the activism of any of these groups – so long as they abided by campus policies and the laws of our commonwealth.

This was my response to the question.

"What office are you running for?" was the reply of the panel moderator.

— • —

It's not uncommon for graduate students in our preparation programs to struggle with questions of personal values being in conflict with the values of their students. Values are an important ingredient in self-definition, though values have a tendency to change over time (not a popular thought to those who have yet to escape a dualistic worldview). As Stephen Covey and others have more recently pointed out, values are merely the roadmap: principles are the actual terrain, and principles are fairly consistent over time. Making the distinction between values and principles should be one of the challenges we put before our graduate interns.

And new staff members.

And long-term staff members.

And ourselves.

Colleges and universities obviously espouse and institutionalize values as central to their constitutions, missions, and practices. Without values, we have no purpose. Let's not confuse our values, however, with political correctness. To me, political correctness is a misnomer and an oxymoron. "Political" implies winning, not necessarily understanding. "Correctness" implies one right answer, not multiple possibilities. Strung together, the two words defy logic. Correct for whom? Political to what end?

Let's look at this idea in the context of students. If we work with student groups or individual students, we have a responsibility to treat them with dignity, equity, and respect, even when we disagree strongly with their ideals and choices.

Our role is to help them develop skills: listening skills to hear other viewpoints; critical thinking skills to help them make informed choices; speaking and writing skills to help them effectively engage in meaningful dialogue; human relations skills to help them effectively interact with people from diverse perspectives and experiences. In this role, we can't afford to wear our own biases, prejudices, political persuasions, and values on our sleeves.

I once knew a mid-level manager in student affairs who was quoted in the campus newspaper as saying, "I can't imagine how any compassionate, thoughtful, intelligent human being could be anything but a Democrat." I have a hard time imagining what credibility this individual subsequently had with students in other political organizations. (Even an aging liberal like me has had the opportunity to work with compassionate, thoughtful, intelligent human beings who were not in the Young Democrats organization.) Bottom line: they're all our students, and they all deserve the same attention, support, and advice from us.

Though frequently attacked from all ends of the political spectrum, the American Civil Liberties Union has learned that liberty and freedom must be protected regardless of the content or context of the ideas in question. If civil liberties are diminished for any one group, it's more likely that civil liberties will be diminished for all groups. If we in higher education give the best of ourselves only to the organizations that represent our personal values, we miss the opportunity to work with some wonderful, energetic, resourceful, diverse individuals.

We lose the chance to learn from them.

I hope the facilitator of that panel discussion so many years ago finally understood that I wasn't running for anything or from anything. I have a number of personal values, but they don't come between me and the students with whom I work. I understand that values can be good or bad. There appears to be honor among thieves, for instance, and the Third Reich had firmly entrenched values. But beyond my values, I operate under a set of principles – translated here as ethics – similar to those practiced by others in our profession (and adopted by the American College Personnel Association in 1985). Ethics are essentially our moral principles put into practice.

I respect autonomy of choice with personal freedoms (of thought, expression, and lifestyle), with the caveat that these freedoms must be universally applied.

I try as hard as I can to do no harm in my work, with the understanding that this includes appreciation of and respect for the faculty, staff, and students with whom I disagree.

I believe that the primary purpose of our profession is to benefit students and the society from whence they came. In fostering the creation of a nation of life-long learners, we benefit others.

I believe in treating our students and their organizations fairly and equitably, with the understanding that justice is a complex issue.

I believe that I can be successful only if I am faithful to my profession, to my institution, to my colleagues, to my students, and to myself.

We must respond to all students and organizations with appreciation for their inherent worth and dignity. We can't play favorites, however 'politically correct' it might seem to do so. We must appreciate diversity, particularly if that's one of the values we hope students will develop.

Even when the goals of the students or groups in question run counter to much of what we believe and perceive, those students or groups should expect that we will treat them fairly. Only when the students or groups incite or engage in illegal or blatantly unethical behavior, violation of institutional policy (which, hopefully, is grounded in ethics and precedent), or disruption of campus programs and services — only then should we act to suspend or redirect their activity, and then in an educationally purposeful manner.

———•———

Easier said than done, right?

No one said that ethics were easy — that's why we have ethical dilemmas.

Each of us in student affairs has the opportunity – and the obligation – to develop the capacity to distinguish between values and principles, and to codify these principles in the form of professional ethics. Ethics are based on core moral principles, not changing personal or political values.

We can identify, articulate, and commit to the principles we find meaningful and then transform these principles into ethical standards through participation in relevant workshops, review of the literature, and personal reflection on our own values and principles. Many professional organizations offer programs on principles and ethics, as do training and development companies and religious organizations. Bookstores and libraries have numerous volumes on principle-centered living and leading and the development of ethical standards based on principles.

I recently asked a staff member to locate at least one learning or training experience each year that would help her identify, articulate, and commit to meaningful principles in her life. I also suggested that she pursue at least one such experience outside the realm of her professional organization. She later thanked me for the opportunity, explaining that the experience far exceeded her expectations and was more useful to her in her work than any of the other professional development experiences she had recently had. She felt she was able to rise above her personal and political values and appreciate leadership as a principle-centered endeavor.

Generally, the organization doesn't require training or development in this area. If not, it's imperative that we as student affairs professionals pursue this training or development independently. We can't put this challenge before others if we haven't addressed it ourselves.

Values have a tendency to change over time; principles are relatively consistent. See if your values are consistent with your principles. Test your ethical standards against your principles. Don't worry about "…what's politically correct on your campus… ." If your values, principles, and ethical standards are coherent, the question will be irrelevant.

REFLECTION

1) Can you distinguish between your guiding principles and your values? How?

2) Are there any groups or individuals on your campus with whom you would rather not interact? Why? What, if anything, can you do to change this situation?

3) How do you teach and model principles/ethics vs. political correctness with your students and staff?

Window Treatments

"For unless they see the sky ...
But they can't, and that is why
They know not if it's dark outside
or light."

BERNIE TAUPIN AND ELTON JOHN

UNLIKE several of my less fortunate colleagues, I've been blessed over the past several years with large windows in my offices. An entire wall was made of glass in my last office. The window wall faced southwest, giving me a morning vista of sunshine on the nearby hillside. Periodically, the angle of the late-afternoon sun was too direct and I had to use the vertical blinds to cover at least a portion of the window. But most of the time, I left the blinds open.

I watched the changing seasons through this window. The spectacular foliage included vivid white and pink blossoms in the spring, lush red and yellow leaves in the fall, an ocean of green in the summer, and somber brown and gray branches against clear blue skies in the winter.

I also watched the changing seasons captured in the apparel and demeanor of the students, staff, and guests who passed by my window. Bright and purposeful in the fall. Bundled up and burdened in the winter. Liberated and buoyant in the spring. Loose and lazy in the summer.

Watching the changing seasons through foliage, apparel, and demeanor gave me a sense of balance and order in the universe — or at least the part of it framed by my window. My window to the world. Something about seeing the outside makes being inside more palatable.

I feel sorry for my colleagues who either have no windows or who have only clerestory windows that let in the light but keep in the sight as well. Sometimes architects can be quite cruel. Their designs frequently result in window pain.

I also feel sorry for my colleagues who work in cubicles. Take away the windows — their computer is the only window to the world they really need. Add bad fluorescent lighting — it's cheaper, and people always work harder under an annoying glare. Install institutional, modular furniture — the kind that takes away any possibility of individual expression. Watch morale go out the window, so to speak.

OK. I realize that not everyone can have a window, and most of us have little choice in determining the location or type of workspace we're assigned. Our buildings, old and new, are likely to have interior and exterior spaces. Finding new ways to get natural light to people or to get people to natural light should be an environmental consideration for all of us. Finding new ways to help people see the outside will make being inside more palatable.

Everyone would benefit from a little window treatment.

We look through windows all the time — in our homes, in our cars, in our buildings. I much prefer the window seat to the aisle seat on the plane; the view doesn't change much inside, but a clear or cloud-filled sky is somehow magical on the outside.

We're drawn to see *what's out there*, even if the weather is threatening and we don't want to go out there. Windows take us beyond our artificial boundaries. Walls without windows are barriers — they keep the inside in and the outside out. Walls with windows are passageways, galleries, conduits, and movie screens where the show never ends — they bring the inside and the outside together.

Seeing the outside makes being inside more palatable.

———•◦•———

We also use windows in a figurative sense.

Window on the world effectively illustrates that we can have only a limited perspective based on where we're sitting or standing. We may see clearly, but we can only see what's visible through our respective window frames. There are endless windows to the world in higher education, limited only by our ability to interact with others.

Window of opportunity is another example. Opportunity is something we can see, out there, but it might not be out there for long. We've got to gather those rosebuds before the season changes. The blinds must be open if we hope to see clearly through our windows of opportunity — otherwise, it might be curtains for us. There are endless windows of opportunity in higher education, limited only by our ability to keep on searching.

Window dressing implies that we're paying more attention to what's on or around the window than we are to what's through the window. We have to be careful not to obscure our view with distractions. Stained glass can be beautiful, but I feel much more spiritual when I can see and experience the natural world, the real world, beyond the illusion.

Window dressings abound in higher education. Perhaps we should limit them by focusing on substance rather than image.

I guess windows are actually doors that we go through with our eyes and our minds. They show where we can go, what we can do, and who we can be. They suggest a world, out there, beyond the walls of our own experiences.

Seeing the outside makes being inside more palatable.

REFLECTION

1) What is your window on the world? Is it wide open or covered by shades?

2) How wide is your window of opportunity? Who controls the window (i.e., who is calling the shots in your life with respect to taking advantage of opportunities, etc.)? Who maintains the window (i.e., who keeps it clean and functional; who is responsible for opportunity in your life)?

3) In what ways does window dressing get in the way of your ability to focus on more important issues and concerns? What can you do to change this?

Pieces of the Past

"Some dreams are made of dust,

And some are meant to last;

The future's always built

On pieces of the past."

R.L.M.

GROWING up in Colorado, I had little opportunity to see structures built prior to the mid 1800s. Mesa Verde was the only place in a several-hundred-mile radius that had any sense of antiquity. The gold mines and ghost towns of the Rockies suggested a bygone era, ephemeral at best, built by people who never really planned on staying after the mother lode was exhausted.

Our architecture was sensible, frugal, utilitarian, built to withstand the long winters, immutable winds, and high-altitude summers of the western plains.

In short, it was pretty boring.

Not until I traveled to the West and moved to the East did I see architecture as cultural, aesthetic, and historical. I experienced firsthand the Spanish charm of the Southwest, the antebellum grace of the South, and the perpendicular power of northern high-rise cities. No picture in a magazine, no panorama in a movie, no television close-up could capture the three-dimensional wonders of architecture, engineering, ingenuity, and imagination. The St. Louis Arch. The Seattle Space Needle. The World Trade Towers. The skyline of Chicago. The quieter, less-traveled streets of New Orleans. The juxtaposition of history and progress in downtown Boston. The Golden Gate Bridge. Rowhouses in Philadelphia and San Francisco. The Mall in Washington, D.C. *People built these things!*

People built colleges and universities as well.

Walking across a college campus is frequently like walking through a beautiful park lined by buildings that have been intentionally brought together physically, philosophically, visually, and functionally. People who don't work on college campuses frequently tell those of us who do just how fortunate we are.

I'm a firm believer in Kurt Lewin's theory (later expanded by James Banning), which suggests that behavior is a function of the person's interaction with the environment. As other researchers confirm, environments cause us to react in terms of approach or avoidance, invitation or rejection, welcome or unwelcome, belonging or not belonging. The values and the mission of the institution should be visible in the physical plant of the institution. There's a transactional relationship in campus ecology. As Winston Churchill once said, "We shape our buildings; thereafter, they shape us."

We teach by what we build.

We also teach by what we destroy.

As a homeowner and a former director of a large university center complex, I realized early in my career that buildings – including homes – are never finished. Renewal, renovation, and expansion are constant considerations. Buildings must change, as the inhabitants' needs change. To influence the design and function of facilities, professionals need to be articulate, if not proficient, in renovation and construction processes. We need to continually modify our facilities to ensure, beyond service delivery, that these facilities provide common ground: bringing people together; minimizing conflict; supporting social interaction; fostering personal growth; honoring the divergent contributions of diverse constituents.

There's a danger, though, in tearing down the old to make room for the new.

> *"Some people see the past and
> want to tear it down,*
>
> *To make a little room for progress
> in their town.*
>
> *A landmark bites the dust,
> and history will fall,*
>
> *Victims of parking lots and
> reckless wrecking balls."*

In the building frenzy that accompanied the rapid growth in higher education following the Second World War — particularly in the 1960s and 1970s — bigger and "better" facilities frequently engulfed or replaced smaller, more modest facilities. The culture and character of earlier times were buried in cinder blocks, concrete, aluminum, and glass. With pressure on campus planners to build the most space possible with available funds, function replaced form.

Out with the old, in with the new.

Living now in Virginia, I've been exposed to the sensitivity of historic preservation. Civic groups band together to prevent fast-food franchises and drive-up "McBanks" from tearing down 200-year-old residences, historic landmarks, and pieces of our collective past. Support for one such group resulted in the lyrics to the song that appears in this essay. Beneath the plastic, vinyl, and alloys of our current age lie the brick, stone, and wood foundations of previous ages.

> *"Some pieces of the past we know*
> *we must preserve,*
>
> *And if we don't act now,*
> *we'll get what we deserve:*
>
> *We'll know just where we are,*
> *but not know where we've been.*
>
> *Memories will die with us and*
> *won't be seen again."*

It's interesting to me that the term "campus ecology" can be interpreted in much the same way as we think of other environments. Preserving aspects of the campus environment may in some ways be as vital as preserving our physical environment. When faced with renovation, renewal, or expansion, we have to begin with the question, "What do we want to save?"

> *"Our era may be judged by*
> *what we didn't save:*
>
> *Our history, our legacy, our cradle,*
> *and our grave;*
>
> *Our water and our air,*
> *our forests and our streams*
>
> *Our landmarks and our land,*
> *and all our other dreams."*

Our students frequently provide leadership in environmental issues. On my campus, it was student interest and activism that resulted in a campuswide recycling effort several years ago. When the campus kiosk — fondly referred to as the "Shroom" because of its resemblance to a large, wooden mushroom — was removed to make way for a new pedestrian plaza, it was student interest and activism that brought the "Shroom" back to the commons. When a new residence hall was being developed, it was student interest and activism that made sure the large trees adjacent to the site would be preserved.

We teach by what we preserve.

We also learn from it.

> *"A building's just a pile of boards*
> *and bricks and stone;*
>
> *A house is just a house,*
> *until you've lost your home.*
>
> *Some dreams are made of dust*
> *and some are meant to last;*
>
> *The future's always built on*
> *pieces of the past."*

REFLECTION

1) What aspects of your campus environment do you wish to preserve? Why?

2) How do your facilities and grounds shape your students, faculty, and staff? How do your students, faculty, and staff shape your facilities and grounds?

3) How do we balance the need for change with the need for preservation?

Passing Stones

"Life flows on within you
And without you."

GEORGE HARRISON

Saturday: 12:30 a.m.

CAN'T seem to get to sleep tonight; a lot on my mind. Important meetings next week on the student success center; worried if people are going to come together. Major institute later in the week on student learning; three presentations and two panels to facilitate. Been looking forward to this for a long time, but I've got to get through those meetings first. Right after the institute is my daughter's graduation open house; looks like it's going to be a busy week.

Ow!

Damn, that hurt. Indigestion? Don't think so. Back pain? No, sciatica doesn't feel like this. Could it be? Don't want to think about that; I've got too much to do next week.

It's not going away. Maybe this will be an easy one. Maybe. I'll get a glass of water and think for a minute. Why now? No use denying it; that sonogram I had a few months ago already revealed its presence. Well, let's get on with it.

"Deb? I hate to wake you, but I'm pretty sure I've got another kidney stone."

Saturday: 1:10 a.m.

Emergency room isn't very busy for a weekend. Wish I could get comfortable somehow. Maybe they'll just give me some medication and send me home; that's always worked before. These things usually take a couple of weeks to pass, and I can generally function at full speed in the meantime. Probably for the best that it happened now rather than during the institute next week. If all goes well, this might be over before then.

IV's hooked up now (didn't hurt much, did it?). Feeling groggy. Sounds like I'll be here through the night. X-rays show what the doctor calls a "moderately large stone"; I asked him to define "moderately large." No response. Just feel like sleeping.

Saturday: 10:20 a.m.

Going home! Feeling all right, with a prescription in case the pain comes back. It's all going to work out. I'll follow up with my doctor early next week. Now I can focus on the meetings, the institute, and the open house. It's great to be home.

Tuesday: 6:45 a.m.

Morning walk was a bit of a grind this morning; I can feel that damn rock again. Maybe I can drown it with cranberry juice. Don't take the prescription unless you really need to. You'll make it. Feeling better already.

Tuesday: 5:20 p.m.

Bad news from Dr. Haley; the stone's too big to pass. Need to follow up with a urologist to see what to do. This thing could still take weeks. Hope I can hold out through the weekend. Got my PowerPoint presentations finished, handouts copied, and a run-through with the equipment behind me. One day at a time. Worried about tomorrow morning's meeting; what can I do to inspire these folks to work together? Change is never easy; we'll get there.

Wednesday: 4:30 p.m.

Meetings went well today; everybody is finally operating like a team. Good plans for the next meeting. Now I can shift gears and focus on the institute; going to be all I do, day and night, for the next four days. Looking forward to making the presentations, participating in the panels, and learning from the other presenters and participants. About 175 people coming to this thing. My sessions won't be quite like the others; going to bring my music background, my English background, and my student affairs background together in a dynamic, creative way. Going to talk about the importance of metaphors in helping others – students and staff – understand and interpret their worlds. Going to talk about the evolution of student activities and the student union, with a focus on the possible "futures" of these entities and their role in learning. Going to present student employment as an incredible opportunity for intentional learning – not merely as an inexpensive means to productivity. Going to talk about change and collaboration. I'm psyched, pumped, primed, and prepared; this could be one of the most fulfilling professional experiences I've ever had. Let the games begin.

Wednesday: 8:15 p.m.

Sunset looks great from my back yard. Just sit here and soak up the solitude for a few minutes. This institute is really important to me; been looking forward to it for months. Great opportunity to share some of my ideas with people whom I admire and respect. Know it's selfish, but I want to do this, not because I've worked hard on the presentations — I want to be one of *them*. Just need to hold out a few more days. So far, so good.

Thursday: 7:30 a.m.

It's back.

With a *vengeance.*

Take one of those pills now. Only last for four to six hours; maybe I'll still make it to the institute faculty meeting this afternoon.

Thursday: 8:30 a.m.

This isn't working.

Lost breakfast, which means I've probably also lost the painkiller. What did the doctor's office say? Call the hospital and ask for the urologist on duty.

He can see me at 10:00?

Thursday: 10:00 a.m.

Really hurts. Want to be a part of the institute. Wish the doctor would hurry; I'm in *pain* here. When should I call Lee and tell him I might have to miss the meeting today? Come on, receptionist, call my name. Nice to have you by my side, Deb; couldn't make it without you. Institute. Pain. Colleagues. Nurses. Why now?

Sick in the examination room. Doctor's seen the X-rays. Recommending surgery today to insert a *stint* in the urinary tract, *lithotripsy* on Saturday, and removal of the stint on Monday. Time to face the facts: I won't be participating in the institute. Disappointment shadowed by pain.

Thursday: 12:25 p.m.

In the hospital now, wearing one of those ridiculous gowns and nothing else. Cold, humiliated, hurting. Feel like crying, but I won't; must be a male thing.

Probably feel better if I did. Typical hospital runarounds: receptionist sent us to the wrong place; nurse couldn't find a vein for the IV; operation scheduled for 12:00, but it's past that time now. This procedure is just preliminary — a stint, the urologist calls it. Invasive, but it will reduce the pain and help the stone fragments pass after they're crushed. Requires full anesthesia, recovery room, observation. Worried: less than two hours ago, I'd never heard of a stint; waivers I've signed indicate the risks involved. Surgery is surgery. Deb called my office; they now know I won't be in for the rest of the week. Guess I can't spend a lot of time worrying about that now; got other things to worry about. Let the games begin.

Thursday: 2:00 p.m.

Bright lights. Kind voices. Familiar face; it's the wife of one of my colleagues, a member of the recovery room staff. Feeling no pain; not feeling much of anything at all. Wasn't I supposed to do something today at 2:00? Oh yeah; the institute faculty meeting. Guess that'll happen without me. Sure put a lot of work into that program. Missed opportunity.

Doctor says he found a second stone when he pushed the first one back into the kidney. Great. Says we'll try to get them both on Saturday. Whatever you say, Doc.

Rolling back to my hospital room. My "roommate" is an older guy, undergoing numerous tests. Probably cancer. Puts everything in perspective for me. Just want to sleep. Noises everywhere; woken up each hour for blood pressure and temperature. Man in the next bed talking to his wife about everything and nothing; can tell he's afraid. Deb sits nearby, working on a quilt that she'll give to our daughter for graduation. Puts everything in perspective for me. Think I'll sleep now.

Thursday: 6:20 p.m.

They're letting me go home for the night! Sleep in my own bed! No blood pressure, no strangers in the next bed, just the comforts of home. Missing the opening session of the institute; guess they'll probably say something about me not being able to present. Uncomfortable; this damn stint is supposed to help? Thank goodness for the advances in modern pharmaceuticals.

Friday: 8:15 a.m.

Time for my first presentation. Let's talk about metaphors, semaphores, and two-by-fours. Opening my eyes to a quiet bedroom. Everything hurts. Things I take for granted – like personal hygiene – take a back seat to pain management. Sure wish I was at the institute. Going to miss the keynote speaker, a wonderful, charismatic woman who's come to talk about invitational education and student success. Going to miss lunch with her. Going to miss the afternoon panel discussion on collaboration. Could be worse; could be in that damn hospital bed. Good day to sleep through. Going to miss that picnic tonight at the university farm; who's going to defend the horseshoe championship?

Saturday: 6:30 a.m.

Checking in at the emergency room for readmittance. Time to crush the stones. Sent off to Second Floor South for a room, this time private. Another gown. Told they won't come for me until 8:30. Two hours to kill. Guess I'll take a nap.

Saturday: 8:40 a.m.

Taking in the ceiling tiles and fluorescent tubes as they roll me across the hospital on the gurney. Small towns like mine get the lithotripsy "van" only once a week. Lucky for me that last Monday was a holiday or I'd be waiting until next Monday for this. Doctors explain the procedure as we wait; important to stay perfectly still; I'll be sedated just to be safe. Won't feel much pain; more like a rubber band snapping on my back. Anesthesiologist asks me a question; don't remember answering. Don't remember the question; I'm presenting my session on transforming the student union into a learning center ...

... In our final exercise, you'll be asked to create a new student union – as a learning center. Your group will be asked to answer these three questions: What would be in it, and why? How would this center/program contribute to student learning? How would this center/program be different than your current student union?

Saturday: 10:00 a.m.

Recovery room again. Familiar faces, familiar sounds. Everything went well, someone says. Welcome back, someone else says. Rolled off to my room. Sure hope people remember to fill out their evaluation forms for the presentation. Need to get ready for that presentation on student employment this afternoon. Could I have another pillow, please?

Saturday: 2:35 p.m.

... And rather than focusing on cheap labor or organizational productivity – although those are both important considerations for all of us – what if we instead saw stint employment as a dynamic setting for learning? Stint employment can be a significant part of a stint's experience at the institution and should be manipulated by the employer to provide a rich opportunity for the acquisition of a variety of attitudes, skills, and knowledge. I'll be back in a minute, just as soon as I fill this jar for the nurse. Oh, and pay no attention to this flimsy gown; I'm fully dressed beneath it ... aren't I? Oh my God!

Saturday: 6:10 p.m.

I fooled them! It was a struggle, but I actually ate some of the hospital food. I know it was just a test; if I didn't eat, they'd say I wasn't ready to go home yet. By eating that soup (what *was* it anyway?) and that awful butterscotch pudding (someone's idea of a joke?), I've indicated that I'm ready to be readmitted to the world. I'm outta here. And to think I could have had dinner tonight with the institute faculty at the Bluestone! There's no justice in the world.

Sunday: 8:45 a.m.

Just one more day of this. Then I can get my life and my body back in order. This morning, the institute ends: I've successfully missed all of it. This afternoon, Chandra's open house happens. I don't want to miss it; better preserve my strength. Focus should be on her, not on me.

Sunday: 5:30 p.m.

Open house went great. Good turnout, though the rain kept us inside. Lots of old friends asking about me; deflect as much as possible. This is about graduation, not operation. Sit, lean, do what you can to get through without looking like someone's old, aging, ailing uncle in the corner. Someone mentions the news that a neighbor from the old neighborhood was at a conference that week, got sick, and ended up in the hospital with a brain tumor.

Puts everything in perspective for me.

Monday: 10:30 a.m.

Ding dong, the stint is gone. Which old stint? The wicked stint!

Take the week off, everybody says. Nothing strenuous for at least a week, the doctor says. Take as much time as you need, the boss says. We'll take care of everything, the office says; just take care of yourself. Puts everything in perspective for me.

Tuesday: 11:30 a.m.

Unlike my hospital roommate or my former neighbor, I was never in any real danger. Kidney stones are commonplace, and even my small town has access to excellent medical resources. I was in good hands throughout: a qualified medical staff, a caring family, a supportive workplace. No, this revelation is not about life and death. It's about perspective.

A child says, "I can't *wait* until my birthday!"

A colleague says, "I can't *afford* to miss that meeting next week."

A student says, "I'm a *failure* if I don't get into med school."

A friend says, "My company will *never* make it without me."

I say, "I've just *got* to make those presentations at the institute."

The birthday will come when it comes; other priorities might make the meeting meaningless; the student may find success and satisfaction in other pursuits; the friend's company – and the friend — may be better off without each other; the institute was just fine, according to all reports.

These stones will pass — painfully sometimes, but they will pass.

I've had several kidney stones over the past twenty years. All but the most recent passed on their own. This last stone – or set of stones – got through to me.

Sometimes your interests, desires, hopes, and aspirations have to be secondary to health, wellness, and life as we know it. This is particularly true when life-threatening issues enter into our consciousness, but perspective is equally important with the more mundane "conditions" that get our attention.

The institute went on just fine without me; it would have also gone on just fine if I'd been there. The university continued to function during my absence; it would have functioned just fine if I'd been there. Puts everything in perspective for me.

These stones will pass.

"Life flows on within you and without you," Mr. Harrison wrote. Not one of my favorite Beatles songs, but an important lesson for me to learn once again. "Life is what happens while you're making other plans," added Mr. Lennon. "I'm taking the time for a number of things that weren't important yesterday," was Mr. McCartney's reply. "What goes on" is about all that Mr. Starr could come up with, but it'll do.

On the bright side, I've got three excellent presentations in the can. If you'd like to know more about metaphors, student employment, or transforming the student union, don't hesitate to contact me.

REFLECTION

1) What are your personal examples of life happening in spite of your plans?

2) What does it take to get your attention? Ultimately, what's most important to you?

3) What's your perspective on perspective?

Dear Chandra

Student affairs is a significant, meaningful, complex, dynamic, and integral component of higher education. I've always known this as a professional — and I now understand it even better as the parent of a college student.

IN this book, I've grappled with reflections on the student affairs profession, both from a professional and a personal perspective. As a professional, I realize that student affairs embodies the institution's responsibility for assisting students as they make the necessary transitions through college and as they develop their own motivation and responsibility for learning. I consider myself fortunate to be engaged on a campus where student affairs is being redefined to better reflect its role in student success, student life, student development, and educational support.

As a parent, I realize that my children will get the most out of their higher education experiences in environments that extend learning beyond the classroom. Student affairs is the intersection of affective and cognitive learning – the arena where skills are honed, knowledge is applied, attitudes are shaped, and competency is developed. Selecting an academic program without regard for the student life program would be akin to selecting a house without considering the neighborhood in which it is located.

What does student affairs mean to *you*? As you continue to wrestle with this question throughout your career, I suggest that you:

- Discover your own *fables*, so that your work will have greater value and deeper meaning for you and for those with whom you work. Think about some of the more consequential incidents or occurrences in your professional life. For each incident or occurrence you identify, answer the following questions: What happened? Why did it happen? What did you learn? How did the experience change your work or your life? These incidents and occurrences are your fables — bring them to life and put them to work.

- Discover – and reframe – the *labels* used to describe you, the labels you use to describe others, and the language we use with varying degrees of effectiveness in our profession. Think about some of the more prevalent labels used in your professional life. For each label you identify, answer the following questions: What does the label actually describe? What is the source of the label (tradition, media, parents, education, etc.)? Does the label help or hurt understanding and communication? Is it possible to improve communication by defining, redefining, or eliminating use of the label? These are your labels — bring them to life and put them to work.

- Discover your own *folding tables* ("tools of the trade") so that you can become more resourceful, more skilled, and more knowledgeable about the needs and expectations of our profession. Think about some of the more significant tools of the trade that you employ in your work (e.g., methodologies, theories, instruments, resources, etc.). For each tool you identify, answer the following questions: What are the properties of this tool (i.e., how and when should it be used and not used)? How competent am I at using this tool, and how could I become more competent? Is this tool well-maintained and ready for use? Do other tools in my professional toolbox complement this tool? These are your folding tables, your tools of the trade — bring them to life and put them to work.

The day after I dropped my daughter off to begin her freshman year, her college career, and a significant new chapter in her life, I wrote the letter that appears below. In this letter, I tried to capture all of the things I wanted to say to her at the pivotal and memorable moment of farewell, when I was rendered uncharacteristically speechless.

It seems fitting to me now that this book would begin with "Sandcastles" and end with this piece, "Dear Chandra." Though close chronologically, the two essays illustrate the powerful emotions, expectations, hopes, fears, and dreams related to the college experience – and therefore to our work as student affairs professionals.

What we do in the student affairs profession is incredibly important. Never forget its importance.

How we do what we do in the student affairs profession is the subject of numerous other publications, and the literature continues to grow every year. Never stop reading about your profession.

Why *we do what we do* in the student affairs profession is perhaps the most important question we could ask of one another and ourselves. This book contains some of my reflections on that question. And this letter, ultimately, is why I do what I do.

———————

> *"And I know I told you I loved you,*
>
> *A thousand and one times I do.*
>
> *But if now I should say*
>
> *'Good luck,' and walk away,*
>
> *Just figure a thousand and two."*

Terry and John Talbot

Dear Chandra,

Yesterday, in a bittersweet moment of joy and sadness, I told you goodbye, leaving you perched on your dormitory loft looking every bit the college freshman. Wearing your college sweatshirt, with class schedules spread out across your comforter, your ceiling and walls dressed up in your personality, you settled into your new life. You were beautiful.

There were a thousand and one things I wanted to say as we left, but I lost the ability to speak. Just like I did when I got married.

Just like I did when you were born.

Somehow I was only able to form the words, "Meet some fun people." Of all the things I could have said, that's the phrase that escaped. I hope you do meet scores of interesting, fun, creative, dynamic people in college. In college, people get to finally decide whom they want to be; that's when they really become interesting, fun, creative, and dynamic human beings. At least some of them.

Go out and meet them because you're one of them.

Of all the things I could have said, I wanted you to know that I couldn't be more proud of you. You worked hard, played hard, and studied hard to get where you are. For the next four years, you'll need to continue working hard, playing hard, and studying hard. It'll be worth it because you get to decide what's important and what isn't, what fits into your life and what doesn't, what's meaningful and what's not. As you learn more and more about the world around you, you'll be surprised how much you also learn about yourself. Work hard, study hard, and play hard. Anything less will leave you dissatisfied.

Of all the things I could have said, I wanted you to know that I'm excited about your future. You have the opportunity to learn in a resource-rich environment. Technology will open many new doors for you that weren't open to my generation. Diversity will expose you to a world of people, ideas, and opportunities that were always there but were not fully understood and appreciated in your parents' time. Knowledge is one of the few things in the human experience that continues to expand, and you'll have the opportunity to know things I never knew. You were raised and educated in one century and you'll live in another. Create the future you desire.

Of all the things I could have said, I wanted you to know that I'll miss you. Your humor and your fresh perspectives. Your warmth and your good cheer. Your thoughtfulness and your compassion. Your love of language and your love of ideas. Your wild and crazy friends. Your gentle way of questioning and challenging. Your sense of justice. Your facial expressions and your personal quirks. The sound of your voice, part little girl and part woman. Part of our farewell was my realization that I was saying goodbye to the little girl I used to pull around in a wagon and hello to the woman you've become.

Of all the things I could have said, I wanted you to know that you'll always have a home even as you create new homes of your own. When the dust settles and you encounter homesickness, realize it's a natural reaction that everyone experiences. Understand that your childhood home is always there should you need it. Knowing it's there sometimes lessens the need. Getting involved in the life of your campus is the very best treatment for homesickness. Let your new life unfold before you, and actively engage in the many experiences you discover. The semester breaks will come faster than you think, and you'll have plenty of opportunities to get a healthy dose of family and old friends. In the meantime, meet some fun people.

Of all the things I could have said, I wanted you to know that I welcome this opportunity to have a new relationship with you. We've taken the parent-child relationship as far as it can go. Now we get to develop an adult relationship, and since you're one of the most fascinating people I know, I look forward to the next phase of our journey. I look forward to being your friend as well as your father.

For years I've stood up in front of parents during summer orientation and talked with them about the changes they'll experience when their son or daughter leaves for college. It was easy for me to tell them that they'd be all right; that the changes would bring mixed emotions that time would help settle; that, ultimately, they would adjust to their new relationship with their students. It was easy for me because I'd never done it. I had it all figured out in my head, but it's that other vital organ that really takes over in times of transition.

Of all the things I could have said, I wanted to say that I love you. I'll miss you. I'm proud of you. I know you're going to do great things. I'll look forward to the times when we'll be together. I'll help you in whatever ways I can.

Do you remember the song I wrote on the day you were born? It ended like this:

> *"My little girl, your hand is so small*
>
> *I'll hold it and guide you*
> *in case you should fall*
>
> *I'll take you to places where*
> *unicorns rule*
>
> *And try to release you when*
> *it's time for school."*

We saw some unicorns, didn't we? It's time for school now. Good luck, my sweet friend. Meet some fun people.

With all my love,
Your Father

Table of "Context": Reflection Questions

The chapter in which the question appears is included in parentheses.

Celebration/Creativity

- If you could create a national holiday, what would you celebrate? ("Private Holidays")

- Are you too busy being too busy to enjoy what you're doing today? (Be honest!) What can you do to change that? ("Private Holidays")

- What potential private holidays could you celebrate? What private holidays might your organization observe? ("Private Holidays")

- What role does imagination play in your organization? In your life? ("Can't You Just Imagine?")

- Has imagination ever gotten you into trouble? Has it ever gotten you out of trouble? ("Can't You Just Imagine?")

- In what activities do you find contrast to your professional work? How do these activities help keep you balanced? ("A New Coat of Paint")

- Which parts of your work have clearcut beginnings and endings? Which parts have neither? Do you prefer the parts with clearcut beginnings and endings or the parts that have neither? Why? ("A New Coat of Paint")

- Does your job have enough stability? Enough creativity? If your job is lacking stability or creativity, how do you compensate for the imbalance? ("A New Coat of Paint")

- How do your facilities and grounds shape your students, faculty, and staff? How do your students, faculty, and staff shape your facilities and grounds? ("Pieces of the Past")

- What are some examples of sandcastles you've built, and what brought them down? ("Sandcastles")

- When *should* sandcastles be protected from the tides? Why? ("Sandcastles")

- How could you use the sandcastle metaphor as a training tool for students or staff? ("Sandcastles")

- Who are the Mr./Ms. B.'s and Mr./Ms. M.'s in your life? What lessons did you learn from each? ("So Close")

- Who are some of the Old Soldiers that influenced your development, and what have they taught you? ("Old Soldiers")

- How have you (or have you?) gone through the stages of appreciation for your Old Soldiers? ("Old Soldiers")

- Are you now, or do you anticipate becoming, an Old Soldier? Why or why not? ("Old Soldiers")

- How do you collaborate with others to achieve student success? How might you collaborate more effectively? ("Transition")

- What are some of the nets on which you rely? Do they help you or hinder you in your work? ("Working Without a Net")

- What treasures do you seek in higher education, either as a worker in higher education, a person pursuing a degree in higher education, or both? ("Treasures")

- How are you pursuing these treasures? ("Treasures")

- Are your treasures somewhere off in the distance or in your proverbial back yard? ("Treasures")

- What is your *window on the world*? Is it wide open or covered by shades? ("Window Treatments")

- How wide is your *window of opportunity*? Who controls the window (i.e., who is calling the shots in your life with respect to taking advantage of opportunities, etc.)? Who maintains the window (i.e., who keeps it clean and functional; who is responsible for opportunity in your life)? ("Window Treatments")

- In what ways does window dressing get in the way of your ability to focus on more important issues and concerns? What can you do to change this? ("Window Treatments")

Change

- Is your organization currently experiencing I-80 conditions or I-70 conditions? ("Auto Biography")

- If you "checked under the hood" of your organization, what would you find? As you did your checking, what would you have in mind: maintenance, or excitement and wonder? ("Auto Biography")

- What two-lane exits are you currently facing, personally or in your organization? In this regard, do you feel you're a traveler, a passenger, a messenger, or a fugitive — that is, how much control of the circumstances do you feel you have, and how is this affecting your choices? ("Auto Biography")

- What role does imagination play in your organization? In your life? ("Can't You Just Imagine?")

- How are ideas, techniques, and technology used in your organization? In your life? How can you apply the "what if" question in both arenas? ("Can't You Just Imagine?")

- Has imagination ever gotten you into trouble? Has it ever gotten you out of trouble? ("Can't You Just Imagine?")

- Which parts of your work have clearcut beginnings and endings? Which parts have neither? Do you prefer the parts with clearcut beginnings and endings or the parts that have neither? Why? ("A New Coat of Paint")

- Does your job have enough stability? Enough creativity? If your job is lacking stability or creativity, how do you compensate for the imbalance? ("A New Coat of Paint")

- What aspects of your campus environment do you wish to preserve? Why? ("Pieces of the Past")

- How do we balance the need for change with the need for preservation? ("Pieces of the Past")

- What are some of the dreams or goals that you've gone beyond? What can you do about it now? ("Ringo, the Packers, 007, and Me")

- Could you, through a better understanding of roles, change your organization to be more real and ideal? If so, how? ("The Role of Roles")

- What are some circumstances in which your role would need to change? ("The Role of Roles")

- What are some examples of sandcastles you've built, and what brought them down? ("Sandcastles")

- When *should* sandcastles be protected from the tides? Why? ("Sandcastles")

- How could you use the sandcastle metaphor as a training tool for students or staff? ("Sandcastles")

- What are your personal examples of life happening in spite of your plans? ("Passing Stones")

- What role does your department play in transition and student success? What, specifically, is your role? ("Transition")

- How do you collaborate with others to achieve student success? How might you collaborate more effectively? ("Transition")

- What are your institution's weaknesses in transition and student success, and how would you, as a parent, expect the institution to address those weaknesses to benefit your daughter or son? ("Transition")

- Should we, in our work, attempt to counter societal messages about winning? If so, how can we do that? ("Winning Isn't Everything")

- What are some examples of won-lost records in student affairs? ("Winning Isn't Everything")

Collaboration/Communication

- How could you best address the questions posed in this essay with a group of students, staff, or peers? ("Collaboration")

- Have you ever lost face and saved something more valuable? ("Collaboration")

- Who are your potential "friends and allies," and how might you collaborate with them? ("Collaboration")

- What are some examples of programs or services you have experienced that were successful in developing multicultural skills, knowledge, or attitudes on the part of students or staff? Why did they work? What are some examples that were unsuccessful? Why? ("Cultural Distinction [What's My Culture?]")

- How can we support those whom we follow, honking encouragement from behind and giving them inspiration so they can find the strength they need to reach collective goals? ("Leading the Gaggle")

- How could you use the notion of "people conditioning" to examine problems with your staff? ("HVAC 101")

- Do you have any magic days that might be seen as arbitrary by your students, co-workers, or peers? If so, what can you do to change that? ("HVAC 101")

- What role does imagination play in your organization? In your life? ("Can't You Just Imagine")

- Are there any groups or individuals on your campus with whom you would rather not interact? Why? What, if anything, can you do to change this situation? ("The Ethics of Political Correctness")

- How do you teach and model *principles/ethics* vs. *political correctness* with your students and staff? ("The Ethics of Political Correctness")

- Who are some of the Old Soldiers that have influenced your development, and what have they taught you? ("Old Soldiers")

- How have you (or have you?) gone through the stages of appreciation for your Old Soldiers? ("Old Soldiers")

- Are you now, or do you anticipate becoming, an Old Soldier? Why or why not? ("Old Soldiers")

- What are some additional examples of labels we use to categorize groups of people, and what are the bases of these labels? ("The Definite Article")

- How would you use the notion of labeling, definite articles, collective nouns, etc., to assist a student or a group of students in overcoming their prejudices? What about staff? ("The Definite Article")

- What labels does your organization tend to use in dealing with its constituents? What can you do to change that? ("The Definite Article")

- How do you collaborate with others to achieve student success? How might you collaborate more effectively? ("Transition")

- What are some of the nets on which you rely? Do they help you or hinder you in your work? ("Working Without a Net")

- Which qualities of an athletic program should student affairs departments emulate? Which qualities should not be emulated? ("Winning Isn't Everything")

- Should we, in our work, attempt to counter societal messages about winning? If so, how can we do that? ("Winning Isn't Everything")

- What are some examples of won-lost records in student affairs? ("Winning Isn't Everything")

Diversity/Culture

- What are some examples of programs or services you have experienced that were successful in developing multicultural skills, knowledge or attitudes on the part of students or staff? Why did they work? What are some examples that were unsuccessful? Why? ("Cultural Distinction [What's My Culture?]")

- What attitudes, awareness, skills, and knowledge do student affairs professionals need that are related to cultural competency? ("Cultural Distinction [What's My Culture?]")

- How would you determine someone's cultural distinction? ("Cultural Distinction [What's My Culture?]")

- How might we more effectively value things, ideas, and people beyond their function? ("Folding Tables")

- How could you use the notion of "people conditioning" to examine problems with your staff? ("HVAC 101")

- Can you distinguish between your *guiding principles* and your *values*? How? ("The Ethics of Political Correctness")

- Are there any groups or individuals on your campus with whom you would rather not interact? Why? What, if anything, can you do to change this situation? ("The Ethics of Political Correctness")

- What are some additional examples of labels we use to categorize groups of people, and what are the bases of these labels? ("The Definite Article")

- How would you use the notion of labeling, definite articles, collective nouns, etc., to assist a student or a group of students in overcoming their prejudices? What about staff? ("The Definite Article")

- What labels does your organization tend to use in dealing with its constituents? What can you do to change that? ("The Definite Article")

- What role does your department play in transition and student success? What, specifically, is your role? ("Transition")

- How do you collaborate with others to achieve student success? How might you collaborate more effectively? ("Transition")

Environment

- Are your surroundings — personal and professional — based primarily on function, form, or both? Why? What are the consequences of favoring one over the other? ("Double Rubs")

- If you were a floor, what type would you be (e.g., wood parquet, wall-to-wall carpet, ceramic tile, wooden planks, carpet tiles, poured terrazzo, sheet vinyl, etc.)? Why? ("Floor Finishes")

- If you had the opportunity and resources, would you change any of the floors in your facilities (literally or figuratively)? Why? ("Floor Finishes")

- What are some of the folding tables/inventions/resources that are critical to your personal and professional success in student affairs? Why? ("Folding Tables")

- Do you have any magic days that might be seen as arbitrary by your students, co-workers, or peers? If so, what can you do to change that? ("HVAC 101")

- How could you use the notion of "people conditioning" to examine problems with your staff? ("HVAC 101")

- How are ideas, techniques, and technology used in your organization? In your life? How can you apply the "what if" question in both arenas? ("Can't You Just Imagine?")

- What aspects of your campus environment do you wish to preserve? Why? ("Pieces of the Past")

- How do your facilities and grounds shape your students, faculty, and staff? How do your students, faculty, and staff shape your facilities and grounds? ("Pieces of the Past")

- How do we balance the need for change with the need for preservation? ("Pieces of the Past")

- What are some examples of sandcastles you've built, and what brought them down? ("Sandcastles")

- When *should* sandcastles be protected from the tides? Why? ("Sandcastles")

- How could you use the sandcastle metaphor as a training tool for students or staff? ("Sandcastles")

- What role does your department play in transition and student success? What, specifically, is your role? ("Transition")

- What are your institution's weaknesses in transition and student success, and how would you, as a parent, expect the institution to address those weaknesses to benefit your daughter or son? ("Transition")

- What are some of the nets on which you rely? Do they help you or hinder you in your work? ("Working Without a Net")

- What is your *window on the world*? Is it wide open or covered by shades? ("Window Treatments")

- How wide is your *window of opportunity*? Who controls the window (i.e., who is calling the shots in your life with respect to taking advantage of opportunities, etc.)? Who maintains the window (i.e., who keeps it clean and functional; who is responsible for opportunity in your life)? ("Window Treatments")

- In what ways does *window dressing* get in the way of your ability to focus on more important issues and concerns? What can you do to change this? ("Window Treatments")

- Which qualities of an athletic program should student affairs departments emulate? Which qualities should not be emulated? ("Winning Isn't Everything")

Leadership

- Does the director title reflect a level of management or a level of leadership at your institution? Do various constituencies (e.g., students, faculty, parents, boards, etc.) have differing perspectives on which role is played by directors? ("Directors")

- How can we teach and model *shared leadership* to prevent our organizations from perpetuating the practice of having one leader at the head of the "V"? ("Leading the Gaggle")

- How can we *keep company with the fallen,* supporting our colleagues and students when they're grounded, regardless of the reason? ("Leading the Gaggle")

- How can we support those whom we follow, *honking encouragement* from behind and giving them inspiration so they can find the strength they need to reach collective goals? ("Leading the Gaggle")

- What role does imagination play in your organization? In your life? ("Can't You Just Imagine?")

- How are ideas, techniques, and technology used in your organization? In your life? How can you apply the "what if" question in both arenas? ("Can't You Just Imagine?")

- Has imagination ever gotten you into trouble? Has it ever gotten you out of trouble? ("Can't You Just Imagine?")

- Can you distinguish between your *guiding principles* and your *values*? How? ("The Ethics of Political Correctness")

- Are there any groups or individuals on your campus with whom you would rather not interact? Why? What, if anything, can you do to change this situation? ("The Ethics of Political Correctness")

- How do you teach and model *principles/ethics* vs. *political correctness* with your students and staff? ("The Ethics of Political Correctness")

- Do you have a recipe for leadership? What are the most important ingredients in your recipe, and why? ("Leadership Recipes")

- How flexible are your recipes? Do you follow the list or improvise? ("Leadership Recipes")

- What's on your plate? Do you have a balanced diet? ("Leadership Recipes")

- Who are the Mr./Ms. B.'s and Mr./Ms. M.'s in your life? What lessons did you learn from each? ("So Close")

- What role do you play in identifying and encouraging the next generation of professionals in your field? ("So Close")

- Who are some of the Old Soldiers that have influenced your development, and what have they taught you? ("Old Soldiers")

- How have you (or have you?) gone through the stages of appreciation for your Old Soldiers? ("Old Soldiers")

- Are you now, or do you anticipate becoming, an Old Soldier? Why or why not? ("Old Soldiers")

- What are some of the nets on which you rely? Do they help you or hinder you in your work? ("Working Without a Net")

- What other circus metaphors (within this essay or from your own imagination) describe your current work situation? How could you use these metaphors as teaching or training tools? ("Working Without a Net")

Organizational Development

- If you "checked under the hood" of your organization, what would you find? As you did your checking, what would you have in mind: maintenance, or excitement and wonder? ("Auto Biography")

- How could you best address the questions posed in this essay with a group of students, staff, or peers? ("Collaboration")

- Does the director title reflect a level of management or a level of leadership at your institution? Do various constituencies (e.g., students, faculty, parents, boards, etc.) have differing perspectives on which role is played by directors? ("Directors")

- What is your perspective on associate or assistant director positions? ("Directors")

- What are some examples of programs or services you have experienced that were successful in developing multicultural skills, knowledge, or attitudes on the part of students or staff? Why did they work? What are some examples that were unsuccessful? Why? ("Cultural Distinction")

- What attitudes, awareness, skills, and knowledge do student affairs professionals need that are related to cultural competency? ("Cultural Distinction")

- What potential private holidays could you celebrate? What private holidays might your organization observe? ("Private Holidays")

- How could you use the notion of "people conditioning" to examine problems with your staff? ("HVAC 101")

- Do you have any magic days that might be seen as arbitrary by your students, co-workers, or peers? If so, what can you do to change that? ("HVAC 101")

- What role does imagination play in your organization? In your life? ("Can't You Just Imagine?")

- How are ideas, techniques, and technology used in your organization? In your life? How can you apply the "what if" question in both arenas? ("Can't You Just Imagine?")

- In your organization, what would people say are your ideal, concealed, and real roles? ("The Role of Roles")

- Could you, through a better understanding of roles, change your organization to be more real and ideal? If so, how? ("The Role of Roles")

- What are some circumstances in which your role would need to change? ("The Role of Roles")

- How could you use the sandcastle metaphor as a training tool for students or staff? ("Sandcastles")

- What labels does your organization tend to use in dealing with its constituents? What can you do to change that? ("The Definite Article")

- What role does your department play in transition and student success? What, specifically, is your role? ("Transition")

- How do you collaborate with others to achieve student success? How might you collaborate more effectively? ("Transition")

- What are your institution's weaknesses in transition and student success, and how would you, as a parent, expect the institution to address those weaknesses to benefit your daughter or son? ("Transition")

- What are some of the nets on which you rely? Do they help you or hinder you in your work? ("Working Without a Net")

- Which qualities of an athletic program should student affairs departments emulate? Which qualities should not be emulated? ("Winning Isn't Everything")

- Should we, in our work, attempt to counter societal messages about winning? If so, how can we do that? ("Winning Isn't Everything")

- What are some examples of won-lost records in student affairs? ("Winning Isn't Everything")

Personal Development

■ What's your double rub potential with respect to work? How durable (emotionally, physically, spiritually) are you? What do you do when you begin to wear down? ("Double Rubs")

■ If you were a floor, what type would you be (e.g., wood parquet, wall-to-wall carpet, ceramic tile, wooden planks, carpet tiles, poured terrazzo, sheet vinyl, etc.)? Why? ("Floor Finishes")

■ What are some of the folding tables/inventions/resources that are critical to your personal and professional success in student affairs? Why? ("Folding Tables")

■ Are you too busy being too busy to enjoy what you're doing today? (Be honest!) What can you do to change that? ("Private Holidays")

■ What potential private holidays could you celebrate? What private holidays might your organization observe? ("Private Holidays")

■ What engenders hope? What engenders fear? ("Hope and Fear")

■ What are your hopes and fears? With whom do you share them? ("Hope and Fear")

■ What's your "chiller"? ("HVAC 101")

■ What role does imagination play in your organization? In your life? ("Can't You Just Imagine?")

■ How are ideas, techniques, and technology used in your organization? In your life? How can you apply the "what if" question in both arenas? ("Can't You Just Imagine?")

■ Has imagination ever gotten you into trouble? Has it ever gotten you out of trouble? ("Can't You Just Imagine?")

■ In what activities do you find contrast to your professional work? How do these activities help keep you balanced? ("A New Coat of Paint")

■ Which parts of your work have clearcut beginnings and endings? Which parts have neither? Do you prefer the parts with clearcut beginnings and endings or the parts that have neither? Why? ("A New Coat of Paint")

■ Does your job have enough stability? Enough creativity? If your job is lacking stability or creativity, how do you compensate for the imbalance? ("A New Coat of Paint")

■ Can you distinguish between your *guiding principles* and your *values*? How? ("The Ethics of Political Correctness")

■ Are there any groups or individuals on your campus with whom you would rather not interact? Why? What, if anything, can you do to change this situation? ("The Ethics of Political Correctness")

- How do you teach and model *principles/ethics* vs. *political correctness* with your students and staff? ("The Ethics of Political Correctness")

- Do you have a recipe for leadership? What are the most important ingredients in your recipe, and why? ("Leadership Recipes")

- How flexible are your recipes? Do you follow the list or do you improvise? ("Leadership Recipes")

- What's on your plate? Do you have a balanced diet? ("Leadership Recipes")

- What are some of the dreams or goals that you've gone beyond? What can you do about it now? ("Ringo, the Packers, 007, and Me")

- What "life internships" have you experienced? How have you dealt with them? ("Ringo, the Packers, 007, and Me")

- What are some examples of sandcastles you've built, and what brought them down? ("Sandcastles")

- When *should* sandcastles be protected from the tides? Why? ("Sandcastles")

- Who are the Mr./Ms. B.'s and Mr./Ms. M.'s in your life? What lessons did you learn from each? ("So Close")

- Who are some of the Old Soldiers that have influenced your development, and what have they taught you? ("Old Soldiers")

- How have you (or have you?) gone through the stages of appreciation for your Old Soldiers? ("Old Soldiers")

- Are you now, or do you anticipate becoming, an Old Soldier? Why or why not? ("Old Soldiers")

- What are your personal examples of life happening in spite of your plans? ("Passing Stones")

- What does it take to get your attention? Ultimately, what's most important to you? ("Passing Stones")

- What's your perspective on perspective? ("Passing Stones")

- What are some of the nets on which you rely? Do they help you or hinder you in your work? ("Working Without a Net")

- What other circus metaphors (within this essay or from your own imagination) describe your current work situation? How could you use these metaphors as teaching or training tools? ("Working Without a Net")

- What treasures do you seek in higher education, either as a worker in higher education, a person pursuing a degree in higher education, or both? ("Treasures")

- How are you pursuing these treasures? ("Treasures")

- Are your treasures somewhere off in the distance, or in your proverbial back yard? ("Treasures")

Professionalism/Professional Development

- How would you distinguish between your *work* (verb) and your *job* (noun)? Are you motivated by your work (what you do) or by your job (office, title, compensation, etc.)? ("Professional Acting")

- If you could create an acting position for yourself, what types of things would you be doing (as opposed to what your title would be, where you would park, what your office would look like, etc.)? How would you act? ("Professional Acting")

- What can you do to give your current position some of the characteristics described above? ("Professional Acting")

- Martyr, mentor, magician, mediator, and mirror: how accurately do these metaphors reflect the role of directors on your campus? ("Directors")

- Does the director title reflect a level of *management* or a level of *leadership* at your institution? Do various constituencies (e.g., students, faculty, parents, boards, etc.) have differing perspectives on which role is played by directors? ("Directors")

- What is your perspective on associate or assistant director positions? ("Directors")

- What are some examples of programs or services you have experienced that were successful in developing multicultural skills, knowledge, or attitudes on the part of students or staff? Why did they work? What are some examples that were unsuccessful? Why? ("Cultural Distinction")

- What attitudes, awareness, skills, and knowledge do student affairs professionals need that are related to cultural competency? ("Cultural Distinction")

- What are some of the folding tables/inventions/resources that are critical to your personal and professional success in student affairs? Why? ("Folding Tables")

- How do hope and fear affect your interactions with those you supervise? Those who supervise you? Your colleagues? ("Hope and Fear")

- What's your "chiller"? ("HVAC 101")

- How are ideas, techniques, and technology used in your organization? In your life? How can you apply the "what if" question in both arenas? ("Can't You Just Imagine?")

- Which parts of your work have clearcut beginnings and endings? Which parts have neither? Do you prefer the parts with clearcut beginnings and endings or the parts that have neither? Why? ("A New Coat of Paint")

- Is your career path a one-way, dead end street? If so, what can you do to change that? And if not, how might you keep it from becoming one? ("Ringo, the Packers, 007, and Me")

- Who are the Mr./Ms. B.'s and Mr./Ms. M.'s in your life? What lessons did you learn from each? ("So Close")

- What role do you play in identifying and encouraging the next generation of professionals in your field? ("So Close")

- In your work with students, particularly student leaders and employees, do you allow them to come close (horseshoes and hand grenades) or do you expect them to be right on target (bulls-eyes)? How do you handle their mistakes? ("So Close")

- Who are some of the Old Soldiers that have influenced your development, and what have they taught you? ("Old Soldiers")

- How have you (or have you?) gone through the stages of appreciation for your Old Soldiers? ("Old Soldiers")

- Are you now, or do you anticipate becoming, an Old Soldier? Why or why not? ("Old Soldiers")

- What are some of the nets on which you rely? Do they help you or hinder you in your work? ("Working Without a Net")

Student Development

- What are some examples of programs or services you have experienced that were successful in developing multicultural skills, knowledge, or attitudes on the part of students or staff? Why did they work? What are some examples that were unsuccessful? Why? ("Cultural Distinction")

- Are there any groups or individuals on your campus with whom you would rather not interact? Why? What, if anything, can you do to change this situation? ("The Ethics of Political Correctness")

- How do you teach and model *principles/ethics* vs. *political correctness* with your students and staff? ("The Ethics of Political Correctness")

- Do you have a recipe for leadership? What are the most important ingredients in your recipe, and why? ("Leadership Recipes")

- How flexible are your recipes? Do you follow the list or do you improvise? ("Leadership Recipes")

- What's on your plate? Do you have a balanced diet? ("Leadership Recipes")

- How could you use the sandcastle metaphor as a training tool for students or staff? ("Sandcastles")

- Who are the Mr./Ms. B.'s and Mr./Ms. M.'s in your life? What lessons did you learn from each? ("So Close")

- What role do you play in identifying and encouraging the next generation of professionals in your field? ("So Close")

- What are some additional examples of labels we use to categorize groups of people, and what are the bases of these labels? ("The Definite Article")

- How would you use the notion of labeling, definite articles, collective nouns, etc., to assist a student or a group of students in overcoming their prejudices? What about staff? ("The Definite Article")

- What labels does your organization tend to use in dealing with its constituents? What can you do to change that? ("The Definite Article")

- What role does your department play in transition and student success? What, specifically, is your role? ("Transition")

- How do you collaborate with others to achieve student success? How might you collaborate more effectively? ("Transition")

- What are your institution's weaknesses in transition and student success, and how would you, as a parent, expect the institution to address those weaknesses to benefit your daughter or son? ("Transition")

- Should our role in higher education be to provide safety nets for our students, or to teach the students so that they don't need nets? ("Working Without a Net")

- Should we, in our work, attempt to counter societal messages about winning? If so, how can we do that? ("Winning Isn't Everything")

About the Author

Randy L. Mitchell is Associate Vice President for Student Success Programs at James Madison University. His current responsibilities include development of the Student Success Learning Center, and the Student Success Services Center.

Prior to his current assignment, Randy served as Acting Associate Vice President of Student Affairs for Enrollment Services (1996-97), Director of the James Madison University Center (1987-96), and Assistant Professor of Psychology (1987-present). Prior to his work at James Madison, Randy served as Program Advisor, Assistant Director, and Associate Director of the Carolyn P. Brown Memorial Union at the University of Tennessee (1978-87).

Randy has a B.A. in English from the University of Northern Colorado (1976) and an M.Ed. in College Student Personnel Administration from Colorado State University (1978). He has worked with student activities, recreation, university centers, leadership development, student media, orientation, admissions, financial aid, registration/records, and student employment, and has been involved with numerous construction projects related to these programs.

Randy has published several articles and conducted numerous presentations on student success, leadership development, service-learning, organizational change, facilities planning and management, role theory, and student employment. His first book, *Metaphors, Semaphores, & Two-by-fours: Reflections on a Personal Profession*, was published in 1997 by the Association of College Unions International.